Einstein noted once that any intelligent fool can make things bigger and more complex, but that it takes a touch of genius—and a lot of courage to boot—to move in the opposite direction. Drawing deeply from the living witness of Christ the King Community Church, Dave Browning does exactly that and in the process gives us a text on a critical subject that is not only highly informative but also inspiring.

—Alan Hirsch, author, *The Forgotten Ways* and *reJesus*, and a founding director of shapevine.com

As the landscape of Christendom changes, most look for new methods, slick fixes, or new forms of church. In *Deliberate Simplicity*, you get something completely unexpected. Dave Browning cuts through all the mess with practical ways to make church natural, simple, and effective. Regardless of the form or stage of your church, *Deliberate Simplicity* will save you time, money, and misery.

—Hugh Halter, author, *The Tangible Kingdom*

I've watched Dave Browning's ministry now for several years, and I'm convinced that what he is doing is one of the most powerful forms of church life I've ever seen. It's a testimony to the fact that size doesn't matter if the church has a God-sized mission. This book not only is worth reading but also is worth keeping on your desk for guidance through a new paradigm of church.

—Bill Easum, www.easumbandy.com

Dave Browning's message of Deliberate Simplicity has important implications for ministries of all sizes. Whether yours is a smaller multiple-campus ministry like Christ the King, a part of the house-church movement, a midsized church, or even a so-called megachurch like the one I pastor, you'll benefit greatly from this penetrating expose of the dangers of complexity, excellence, overcaution, and the goofy idea that bigger is somehow always better.

—Larry Osborne, North Coast Church

DELIBERATE SIMPLICITY

The Leadership Network Innovation Series

The Big Idea: Focus the Message, Multiply the Impact, Dave Ferguson, Jon Ferguson, and Eric Bramlett

Confessions of a Reformission Rev.: Hard Lessons from an Emerging Missional Church, Mark Driscoll

Leadership from the Inside Out: Examining the Inner Life of a Healthy Church Leader, Kevin Harney

The Monkey and the Fish: Liquid Leadership for a Third-Culture Church, Dave Gibbons

The Multi-Site Church Revolution: Being One Church in Many Locations, Geoff Surratt, Greg Ligon, and Warren Bird

Sticky Church, Larry Osborne

DELIBERATE 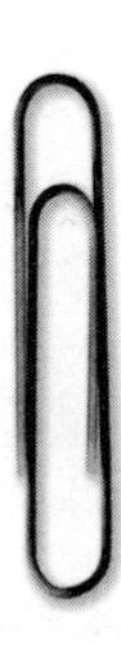 SIMPLICITY

How the Church Does More by Doing Less

DAVID BROWNING

ZONDERVAN.com/
AUTHORTRACKER
follow your favorite authors

Deliberate Simplicity

This title is also available as a Zondervan ebook. Visit www.zondervan.com/ebooks.

This title is also available in a Zondervan audio edition. Visit www.zondervan.fm.

Requests for information should be addressed to:

Zondervan, *Grand Rapids, Michigan 49530*

Library of Congress Cataloging-in-Publication Data

Browning, Dave, 1964-
Deliberate simplicity : how the church does more by doing less / Dave Browning.
p. cm.
ISBN 978-0-310-28567-0 (softcover) 1. Church growth.
I. Title.
BV652.25.B77 2009
253—dc22 2008033724

Interior design by Melissa Elenbaas

Printed in the United States of America

---

08 09 10 11 12 13 • 21 20 19 18 17 16 15 14 13 12 11 10 9 8 7 6 5 4 3 2 1

CONTENTS

Preface 9

Acknowledgments 13

Introduction to a New Equation 15

1. Minimality 35
2. Intentionality 65
3. Reality 93
4. Multility 125
5. Velocity 151
6. Scalability 175

Conclusion: It's an Equation 199

Notes 203

PREFACE

I'm a pastor ... again.

When I quit in the midnineties, I was unsure about a lot of things, but one thing was clear: I would never be a pastor again.

God had other ideas. While I had quit on him, he never quit on me. He led me into green pastures and beside still waters. He restored my soul. I found myself in the back row of a nondenominational church in Bellingham, Washington.

At Christ the King Community Church I found love, acceptance, and forgiveness. In that safe and sane environment, God began to heal my pain and rekindle my passion. During those days of restoration, a prayer partner exhorted me, a pastor mentored me, and a congregation supported me. After serving as an associate pastor for several years, I was ready to "get back on the bike." On Easter Sunday, April 4, 1999, I launched Christ the King Community Church of Skagit Valley, a daughter church which in two years grew to a thousand people meeting in hundreds of homes and several communities. In the ensuing years, CTK has become a minimovement with branches across the country and overseas.

So I'm a pastor again, but it's not the same. I'm not the same, to be sure. But the context in which I'm ministering is also quite different. *Deliberate Simplicity* is an attempt to describe these differences.

More than one audience may benefit from *Deliberate Simplicity*:

1. The people of Christ the King Community Church, or any church for that matter, who are the real ministers. *Deliberate Simplicity* is designed to prepare them for their work.

Because we are surrounded by tens of thousands of lost people, there is an urgency about our mission. The harvest is great. We do not have time to wait. We want to reach as many people as we can, as fast as we can. Hopefully, this handbook will speed the process of deploying the next generation of ministers for the harvest.

2. The leaders of CTK, or of any church, who are the "administers." As caretakers of the mission, vision, and values of Christ the King, it is their mandate to create and sustain an environment where the people of CTK can execute their ministries with minimum obstacles and maximum fulfillment. *Deliberate Simplicity* is a handbook to this end. Because we are a multilocation church and hope to expand into thousands of sites, we can no longer leave the handoff of our DNA to oral tradition or to chance.
3. The disillusioned minister (lay or pay) who may have given up on church but not on God. If you have become disenchanted with BAU (business as usual) in the church, a new mental model may invigorate your passions. It has had that effect for me and many others.

Laced throughout <u>Deliberate Simplicity</u> are essay questions. These questions may be used to facilitate a discussion with a mentor or group, or for personal journaling. Here's the first one:
Of the three audiences mentioned above, which include you, if any? Explain.

While I am excited about this different approach to ministry, I hope to steer clear of elitism. Different does not necessarily mean better. While at times I may contrast the Deliberately Simple church with the traditional church, *Deliberate Simplicity* is intended to be more descriptive than proscriptive. God is at work in every church, and in every church tradition there are elements that work well for the people in those traditions. We all have to be faithful to what God is calling us to be and do. Our loyalty should be to the Master and the mission, not the method and the manner. My choosing to go a different direction is not an indictment of those who may be comfortable where they are. I mainly want you to know that this path is out there and that you can take it if you'd like.

While I was growing up in Alaska, my dad would take me with him on fly-in fishing trips. As we walked through the trees from the landing strip to the river, my dad would sometimes take pieces of brightly colored ribbon and tie them in the tree branches. These ribbons would prove valuable later when it came time to walk back to the plane, but also if some fishing buddies wanted to join us. We'd just tell them, "Follow the ribbons from the airstrip." Admittedly, the path of church ministry that I am on is not well worn. But the enjoyment should be spread around. I'm tying some ribbons in the trees so you can find your way if you want to join us. The fishin's good.

I'm also acutely aware that results may vary. Just when you say the fishin's good, your friends show and can't get a bite. There are aspects of the CTK story that are mysterious and defy explanation. The exponential growth of CTK is certainly a God thing. We are clear on this point. God has been extraordinarily gracious and kind to us, and if he were ever to withdraw his hand of blessing, our ministry would fall like a house of cards. To God be the glory; great things he has done.

However, it does appear that the CTK story has been a divine-human partnership. We couldn't do it without God, but God has also chosen not to do it without us. And we have worked hard to cooperate with God. The seeming ease of growth at CTK belies the hard work and discipline that has made it possible. A maxim with which CTK leaders have become well versed is, "There is no growth without change, no change without loss, and no loss without pain." There are some extremely dedicated, disciplined leaders at CTK who have paid the price for those who are about to come.

Describe your church experience to this point. What churches have you attended? What denominations have you experienced? Has the fishin' been good?

The success of CTK is a credit to the genius of the Holy Spirit. We have been given a different conceptual framework with which to work, and we are thankful. We are going to share those ideas here in the form of an equation.

God bless you,

—Dave Browning
Burlington, Washington
dave@deliberatesimplicity.com

ACKNOWLEDGMENTS

I'm indebted to many colleagues and authors who have stimulated my thoughts over the years, and whose ideas are now going to be a part of this stew.

The meat and potatoes are compliments of Steve Mason, the founding pastor of Christ the King Community Church in Bellingham, Washington. Steve passed on the basic recipe that will be articulated here.

I'm going to spice freely from some of my favorite authors. There is much in business, science, and technology that is analogous to the Deliberately Simple church. When it comes to great ideas, you'll soon find that I am into not manufacturing but distribution. Hopefully, there's been value added along the way.

The prep work for this dish was a labor of love executed by a number of assistants over a span of fifteen years: Jurrell "MC" McCrory, Carmielle "CC" Cox, Penny "Not Less" Moore, Jan "The Loose" Cannon, Cheri "Oteri" Milhomme, Christina "Visalli" Archer, Donna Gremmert, Hilary "HB" Bonnette, and Diana LaSalle. Each diced and sliced over a hot photocopier. Thank you.

Thanks to my associate taste testers. Valuable support and encouragement came from my family and friends. Among those who sipped from the wooden spoon are my parents and my pastor-colleagues in the CTK network. I fed them bits and pieces along the way, and their feedback impacted flavor.

Finally, thanks to God for not giving me what I deserve, to my wife, Kristyn, for loving me so well, to my three kids, Erika, Jenna, and Daron, for the privilege of being their dad, and to the people of Christ the King for walking the talk.

Bon appétit!

INTRODUCTION TO A NEW EQUATION

A NEW EQUATION

Imagine with me for a minute ... a church ... but not your typical church. A church where the main thing is the main thing. A church where people convene primarily in homes and secondarily in public spaces for worship services. A church where the ministry is carried out by ordinary people, and it is the pastor's job to identify, deploy, train, and support these ministers. A church that is warm and accepting of both the churched and the unchurched. A church that sees hundreds of converts baptized each year. A church that numbers tens of thousands but convenes in thousands of small groups and scores of small worship centers. A church that has no geographical limits but spreads from house to house, neighborhood to neighborhood, town to town, county to county, state to state, and country to country. A church that is not just multilocation but also multiethnic and multinational.

What if this church were intentionally structured to reach an unlimited number of people in an unlimited number of places? What if this church were more like a movement than a ministry?

Do you have this picture in your mind? For me it's not too difficult to imagine. I've been living inside this picture for the last few years.

Christ the King Community Church held its first worship service on Sunday evening, April 4, 1999, in Mount Vernon, Washington. In May of that year, CTK began to hold morning services, going to two services in September and three services the following February. During its first year, Christ the King of Skagit Valley grew at a rate of 12 percent a month to an average of over 500 people per week, with a high attendance of 763. By the end of CTK's first year, thirty-eight small groups were convening weekly in Jesus' name for friendship, growth, encouragement, and outreach.

From 2000 to 2004, CTK established hundreds of small groups throughout the region, with worship centers located in ten cities, in four counties. In 2004, *Outreach Magazine* recognized CTK as one of the fastest-growing churches in America.

In 2005, CTK began to expand across the country and around the world. We are now poised to go as far as relationships will take us (a current list of locations can be found online at www.ctkonline.com). CTK has experienced extraordinary results by keeping it simple.

Church growth in the seventies, eighties, and nineties was defined by the megachurch. As researcher George Barna says, "We live in an era of hyperbole. Everything is supersized, global, mega-this, and biggest-ever-that. Even the religious community has succumbed to the world's infatuation with size. The pinnacle of church success is to become a megachurch." Megachurches have proven they are able to reach thousands of people with burgeoning budgets, sprawling campuses, huge payroll, and extensive programming. Large churches have demonstrated for the past three decades that more can be more. Deliberate Simplicity is a new equation for church development. It says less can also be more. This represents a paradigm shift.

When the paradigm shifts, the rules change. In baseball, for example, the foul lines are part of the paradigm. If the ball lands on one side of the line, it's a fair ball. If it lands on the other side of the line, it's a foul ball. If the ball is hit over the fence, it's a home run. If it lands short of the fence, it's playable. What accounts for these differences? The paradigm. A paradigm is a set of rules that tell you how to play the game in order to be successful.

When I say that Deliberate Simplicity is a new paradigm for the church, I'm saying the lines have been moved from where you might expect to find them in a traditional church. "Traditional church" may sound pejorative. Here we mean simply a church defined by its locale, programs, facility, or denomination. If you hear someone say,

- "I attend the (color or architecture) church at the corner of Maple and Division"
- "My family has been members of the (Denomination) Church for generations"
- "I really like the productions they do over at the (First Something) Church"
- "Have you seen the new education wing the (big church in town) built?"

they are probably talking about a traditional church.

In the Deliberately Simple church, the rules are: "Less is more, and more is better." Success within these lines boils down to six factors, presented here in the form of an equation: $< = - \times + \infty$.

Factor	Symbol	Objective	Question
Minimality	<	Keep it simple.	What
Intentional-ity	=	Keep it mis-sional.	Why
Reality	–	Keep it real.	How

Multility	×	Keep it cellular.	Where
Velocity	+	Keep it moving.	When
Scalability	∞	Keep it expanding.	How Far

The main ideas of Deliberate Simplicity are outlined in six sections. The first three (minimality, intentionality, reality) explain how less is more. The last three (multility, velocity, scalability) expand on how more is better. The modular approach I have taken to writing about Deliberate Simplicity mirrors the modular approach we have taken in ministry. Each of the six chapters can stand on its own but is also part of a greater whole.

The differences between a Deliberately Simple church and a traditional church need to be discussed, because when you are in the middle of a paradigm, it is sometimes hard to imagine any other paradigm. Upside Down Map Co. of Derby, England, recently teamed up with Map Link Inc. of Santa Barbara, California, to print a road map of California with north and south reversed to make map reading easier for drivers heading south. Why didn't I think of that? Probably because I was stuck in a paradigm that says a map always has to be laid out with N pointing up. When you get out of the box, you can see new possibilities.

Fifty years ago a church "map" invariably involved a church with a steeple, a seminary-trained minister in a three-piece suit or robe, a pew-filled sanctuary, hymnals, an organist, and a sermon delivered from behind a wooden pulpit. Today, if you participate in a Deliberately Simple church, you will most likely meet in a rented auditorium, sit on a stackable chair, sing along with projected lyrics and a rock band, and hear conversational teaching by a bivocational pastor in blue jeans sitting on a stool.

Church growth expert Peter Wagner speculates that the number of churches that are out of the box now exceeds the amount of churches in the largest Protestant denomination, which has around forty thousand churches nationwide. Donald Miller, professor at the University of California at Berkeley, outlines twelve characteristics of the "New Paradigm Church":

1. They were started after the mid-1960s.
2. The majority of the congregation members were born after 1945.
3. Seminary training of clergy is optional.
4. Worship is contemporary.
5. Lay leadership is highly valued.
6. They have extensive small group ministries.
7. Clergy and congregants usually dress informally.
8. Tolerance of different personal styles is prized.
9. Pastors tend to be understated, humble, and self-revealing.
10. Bodily, rather than mere cognitive, participation in worship is the norm.
11. The gifts of the Holy Spirit are affirmed.
12. Bible-centered teaching predominates over topical sermonizing.[1]

Of the twelve characteristics, which three do you believe have special importance?

The church has always undergone change, reformation, and revolution. But today the major reforms taking place in the church are in the area of methodology rather than message, in practice more than theology. According to church growth expert Peter

Wagner, "The radical change in the sixteenth century was largely theological. The current reformation is not so much a reformation of faith (the essential theological principles of the Reformation are intact), but a reformation of practice." Yet for the church—which often institutionalizes its practices—reforms in methodology can prove every bit as epic as reforms in theology. Fortunately, the significant changes that used to take decades, if not centuries, for the church to embrace are now happening in months and years.

One of the chief practical advantages of the Deliberately Simple paradigm is the speed at which gains can be achieved. If the goal is to build Christ's kingdom and see spiritual transformation happen on a massive scale, then the traditional church is not going to get it done. We are winning some battles but losing the war. In the United States, for instance, while megachurches are getting bigger and bigger, the culture is becoming more and more secular. In the Two-Thirds World, to which the "bigger is better" paradigm has been exported, the monetary requirements of building buildings and supporting pastors has been stifling and stalling the church. Only middle- to upper-class communities (or ministries supported from the outside) can pay the bill for the properties and staff they "need." Instead of focusing on outreach, the church spends excessive energy focusing on the money it feels it requires to do outreach.

Deliberately Simple churches are finding that the way to effect dramatic change is to change the rules. When you change the rules, you automatically change the roles and results.

	Traditional	**Deliberately Simple**
Goal	Improvement	Redefinition
Focus	Behaviors and Rules	Attitudes and Roles

Risk	Low	High
Result	Minor Gains	Major Gains
Speed	Slow	Fast

Sometimes the paradigm you're working with does more harm than good. For instance, the prevailing medical theory used to be bloodletting. Now it's germ theory. What if hospitals had done TQM (total quality management) on bloodletting? They would have been doing the wrong thing even better. If the paradigm doesn't work, executing the paradigm better actually makes things worse. You climb the ladder only to find that it's leaning against the wrong wall.

While I agree with the axiom that says, "No model is perfect; some are useful," there is a growing sense that the megachurch ladder may be leaning against the wrong wall. In fact, the situation may be more dire than that. In his book *Revolution*, researcher George Barna speaks to a growing angst regarding the institutional church. His research indicates that there may be as many as twenty million spiritual revolutionaries who no longer view the church as the locus for their spiritual experience. Church consultant Reggie McNeal states that "a growing number of people are leaving the institutional church for a new reason. They are not leaving because they have lost faith. They are leaving the church to preserve their faith."

When decidedly different, more useful answers to questions start to appear, you are seeing the beginnings of a new paradigm. With momentum, these new rules become a paradigm shift. The Deliberately Simple church appears to be in the same place in its development as the United States of America prior to the Constitutional Convention in Philadelphia. We have a dream. We have a new land in which to live out that dream. We have principles that are guiding us. We are experiencing newfound freedom living by these principles. To facilitate further expansion, we have to do what the Founding Fathers did. We have to put our hearts on parchment. As Martin Luther nailed ninety-five theological tenets to the church door in Wittenberg, today we are posting this practical thesis in big, bold letters: **DELIBERATE SIMPLICITY**.

The word *Deliberate* says that we want to be intentional about what we try to do and how we try to do it.

> **de•lib•er•ate** *adj*: carefully thought out and done intentionally

By definition, *deliberate* speaks to design ("thought out") as well as drive ("done intentionally"). A deliberate church thinks through the outcomes it wants to achieve, lets form follow function, and takes responsibility for results.

Simplicity describes the manner in which the Deliberately Simple church intends to carry out its mission: simply.

By simple we mean:

> **sim•ple** *adj* ***sim•pler, sim•plest*** **1:** easy to understand, deal with, use, etc.: *a simple matter; simple tools* **2:** plain; not elaborate or artificial: *a simple style* **3:** unadorned; not ornate or luxurious: *a simple gown* **4:** unaffected; unassuming; modest: *a simple manner* **5:** not complicated: *a simple design* **6:** single; not complex or compound **7:** occurring or considered alone; mere; bare: *the simple truth; a simple fact.* **8:** free from deceit or guile; sincere; unconditional: *a frank, simple answer* **9:** common or ordinary: *a simple soldier* **10:** unpretentious; fundamental: *a simple way of life* **11:** humble or lowly: *simple folk*
>
> **syn 1:** clear, intelligible, understandable, unmistakable, lucid **2:** plain, natural, unembellished, neat **3:** unpretentious

In the book of Acts, we find the first-century church meeting in homes and gathering in public spaces for assembly. The

Looking at the above definitions, how do you feel about the words simple and church going together?

early church was not about religion but about relationships ... loving God with all your heart, soul, mind, and strength and loving your neighbor as yourself. It was that simple. Deliberate Simplicity inquires, "Can't we go back to that?"

THE BANE OF COMPLEXITY

Complexity has been a prevailing trend in modernity, but people are not wired for it naturally. One of the reasons your phone number has seven digits is that Alexander Graham Bell conducted studies that indicated that retention fell off dramatically beyond seven numbers. Psychologist George Miller wrote a famous paper in the 1950s entitled "The Magic Number Seven Plus or Minus Two." Miller's studies showed that people can handle only about seven pieces of information at any one time in their short-term memory.

Studies are showing that we get bogged down when we have too many "open circuits." Educators are finding that when it comes to the brain, less is more. Parents who overstimulate their young children are missing the point. Author John Bauer, in *The Myth of the First Three Years*, says it is not about having more synaptic connections. It's about capitalizing on the strongest connections. In fact, many billions of connections will be shut down naturally so you are freed up to exploit the ones that remain. Biologically, losing connections is the point, not gaining them.

When I was a kid in Alaska, we had only three or four television channels (yes, and I really do have stories about walking to school in the snow too). With so few channels, I pretty much had the programming memorized for the entire week. Those days are long gone. Today there are so many channels, so many programs, so many publications, so many websites, that we will all feel hopelessly behind unless we are deliberate about our simplicity. Absorbing all the data is impossible. The sooner we filter the channels, the better.

People are growing to not just desire simplicity but demand it. An anonymous email comes to Google (a leading search engine on the internet) on an ongoing basis. Every time, the email contains only a two-digit number. It took the folks at Google a while to figure out what the author was communicating. He was giving them feedback on the number of words on Google's homepage. When the number started to go up, say to fifty, he would get agitated and send them an email. Now Google finds his emails helpful, because his feedback has disciplined them to not introduce too much complexity on their homepage. The email is like a scale for words.

In contrast, rival web portal Yahoo! has over five hundred words on its homepage. Its model of "ministry" is more akin to the modern megachurch—providing a multitude of links and options for its users.

> Yahoo! is about everything, so it is forgivable to think that it may stand for nothing. . . . Google is a classic example of succeeding through focus and execution. Yahoo!'s model, by comparison, is anything but classic. The company's offerings are so broad that it isn't considered the go-to site for any particular service or feature.
>
> —Michael Malone

Both Yahoo! and Google are successful in attracting visitors to their sites (119 million per month and 72 million per month, respectively) and have strong revenue ($3.2 billion and $2.7 billion). But while Yahoo! is proving that more can be more, Google is proving that less can be more. Google's style in advertising is minimalist. Yet the little text-only ads on Google outperform the flashy, full-page banners on Yahoo!

While the "less is more" approach hasn't received much play in the church, it has been catching on for a while in business. For instance, In-N-Out Burger, a California-based chain of 175 burger joints, has a business model similar to Google's. It is Deliberate Simplicity applied to food service. The company draws lunchtime crowds with its few offerings. It sells burgers—single or double—fries, sodas, and shakes. That's it. Cheese is one of the few options. By contrast, McDonald's has added thirty-seven items to its core menu since 1955.

Warehouse retailer Costco takes a deliberately simple approach. They offer fewer choices in larger packaging. That means some customers may pass up purchases because the gallon jar of mayonnaise is too big or the brand isn't their favorite. But the benefits far exceed the lost sales. Stocking fewer items streamlines distribution and hastens inventory turns—and nine out of ten customers are perfectly happy with the mayonnaise. Costco's warehouses are spartan (concrete floors, fluorescent lighting, etc.). Their pricing displays are understated (paper in a plastic sleeve). They stock less than 10 percent of the items of a typical Wal-Mart. They are very selective in what they choose to offer. Yet Costco is doing just fine, and Wal-Mart is trying to emulate their success with their Sam's Clubs.

In office supplies, Deliberate Simplicity is the difference between Staples and Office Depot. Staples wants to make it easy. They feature "the easy button" in their promotions. Their goal is to make it easy for you to get in and get out quickly. Office Depot wants you to stay around and shop.

Trader Joe's is a specialty grocery retailer that has become a cultural phenomenon by keeping it simple. Len Lewis, in his book *The Trader Joe's Adventure*, says,

> Because Trader Joe's has mastered operational disciplines that elude even the most sophisticated retailers, many retail industry experts say the chain defies any neat description or

> standard categorization. By all rights, the very things that make it successful should be a recipe for disaster. Its average store is only about half the size of even the smallest neighborhood supermarket these days. Each location only carries about 2,500 items, compared to an average of 25,000 at conventional supermarkets. And instead of large, easy-to-access locations, most are housed in relatively small, older strip shopping centers with limited parking.... [Yet by] being different, Trader Joe's has built itself into a business with annual sales of $2.6 million, or $1300 per square foot, which is about twice the supermarket industry average.... From the beginning, the company's guiding principle was to offer a limited number of items at extremely low prices in barebones stores.[2]

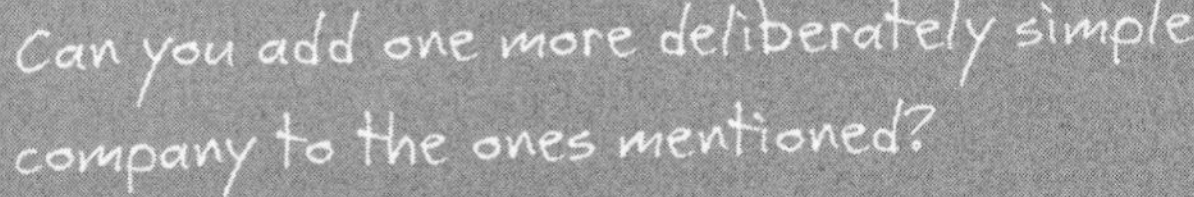

USA Today recently ran a front-page cover story heralding "our national craving for all things simple." We've got cell phones, pagers, Palm Pilots, and iPods. But a recent poll found that nearly one in five Americans are seriously seeking alternatives to their hectic daily lives. The desire for simplicity is an age-old yearning that is being exacerbated by "technological progress." If you don't believe this, try counting the money the Chicken Soup for the Soul books have made, or looking into the resurgence of National Public Radio.

> We live in a world much akin to the first century. The acids of modernity have eaten away our sophistication, and we are stripped down to the nakedness of simplicity.
>
> —Jess Moody

Simplicity works better than complication partly because it mitigates the impact of Murphy's Law. U.S. Air Force Captain Edward Murphy said in 1949, "Anything that can go wrong, will go wrong." Mathematicians have now come up with factors that increase the likelihood of Murphy's Law coming into play, like urgency, complexity, importance, and skill. From running different scenarios, they found that to increase the odds of disaster, all you need to do is combine two of the above elements. For instance, try to avoid doing anything complex when you're in a rush. Or, as we have espoused in Deliberate Simplicity, when you have something important to do, keep the process simple. The more complexity in the system, the more likely that implementation will fail. Some churches are living examples of this. Why are things always going wrong? Murphy's Law, amplified by complexity. The law of complexity says that the level of complexity is equal to the square of the number of different steps in a task.

> We were 1-2 and we were running forty-seven plays on offense. I cut that to thirteen and we won four in a row.
>
> —Lou Holtz, Football Coach

> One of the things that made Wendy's better was putting a limit on the number of ideas we would implement.
>
> —Dave Thomas, Founder of Wendy's

Eric Bende spent eighteen months off the power grid with the Minimites—a group who decided to go without telephones, running water, refrigeration, or electricity. He wrote about his experiences in *Better Off: Pulling the Plug on Technology*. His conclusion was not that technology is a problem but that letting technology dominate our lives is. Bende advises, "When in doubt, use less technology."

One of the questions that takes the church back to basics is, how would we do church if we didn't have electricity? Your answer will undoubtedly push you back to the essence of the church and away from the artificiality of modernity. I like Matthew 10:9–10 in *The Message*: "Don't think you have to put on a fund-raising campaign before you start. You don't need a lot of equipment. *You* are the equipment." Like Henry David Thoreau, I believe that "technology has become an improved means to an unimproved end." One of our CTK pastors encourages the people in his worship center to occasionally fast from technology (no phones, TV, lights, etc.) for personal health.

Most of our CTK worship centers utilize an overhead projector to show song lyrics, instead of computer-driven PowerPoint. Why? It's relatively inexpensive to get set up with a projector. It's relatively simple to prepare and execute. Anyone can operate the equipment. It is a low-tech, simple solution. We're not trying to dazzle people with pixels. We're not trying to impress them into the kingdom of God. We're attempting to love them in. For the most part, the service order you'll find at a CTK worship center consists of two parts: uninterrupted worship and very clear, lucid teaching, with no bells or whistles.

Technology doesn't always work for us like we think it does. Sometimes technology is a waste of time. A study of boardroom decision-making determined that the same decision would have been made whether or not there was a fancy PowerPoint presentation. While computers can be very helpful (particularly to speed up and automate laborious processes), they also give us the capability to play solitaire, send instant messages, fiddle with fonts or monkey around with layout, all of which is dissipated waste.

Sometimes technology works against you by making things more difficult instead of less. Jim Collins, in *Good to Great*, uses the conflict in Vietnam as a case in point.

> Technology cannot turn a good enterprise into a great one, nor by itself prevent disaster. History teaches this lesson repeatedly. Consider the United State's debacle in Vietnam. The United States had the most technologically advanced fighting force the world has ever known. Super

> jet fighters. Helicopter gunships. Advanced weapons. Computers. Sophisticated communications. Miles of high-tech border sensors. Indeed, the reliance on technology created a false sense of invulnerability. The Americans lacked, not technology, but a simple and coherent concept for the war on which to attach that technology. It lurched back and forth across a variety of ineffective strategies, never getting the upper hand.
>
> Meanwhile, the technologically inferior North Vietnamese forces adhered to a simple, coherent concept: a guerrilla war of attrition, aimed at methodically wearing down public support for the war at home. What little technology the North Vietnamese did employ, such as the AK-47 rifle (much more reliable and easier to maintain in the field than the complicated M-16), linked directly to that simple concept. And in the end, as you know, the United States—despite all its technological sophistication—did not succeed in Vietnam.[3]

The current war on terrorism is taking us back to a "less is more" approach.

> On September 11, 2001, a tiny band of Internet-savvy fundamentalists humbled the world's only superpower. It turned out that the FBI, the CIA, a kiloton of tanks, and an ocean of aircraft carriers and nuclear subs were no match for passionate focus, coordinated communication, and a few $3.19 box cutters. The terrorist conceived the ultimate "virtual organization"—fast, wily, flexible, determined. And then, despite numerous slip-ups, said terrorists trumped the bureaucratic behemoths lined up against them.
>
> —Tom Peters, *Re-imagine*

Shortly after the September 11 attacks, Defense Secretary Donald Rumsfeld, discussing the search for Osama Bin Ladin, asked rhetorically, "Is it likely that an aircraft carrier or a cruise missile is going to find a person?" Obviously, to find individuals hiding in caves, the strategy will have to be much more pedestrian.

Deliberate Simplicity is a "boots on the ground" approach to the church's mission. We believe that if we can get God's people to simply love God and love people, the church cannot be stopped.

THE COMPLICATED CHURCH

In the absence of Deliberate Simplicity, churches can easily become complicated, either in message (theologically) or in method (organizationally). I've experienced both the complication that comes from too many doctrines and the complication that comes from too many programs.

I was raised in a traditional church—a church that was decidedly denominational and conservative. The particular denomination in which I grew up had emerged from the theological conflicts of the early twentieth century, when liberalism began to challenge the inerrancy of Scripture. As believers were separating from this heresy and apostasy, a particular group of churches decided to practice second-degree separation—to extricate themselves not only from heretics but also from anyone who did not separate from heretics. This quest for extreme purity, while well-meaning, spawned a culture of guilt-by-association, suspicion, judgmentalism, and legalism. Over the decades, more issues surfaced, more lines were drawn, and more doctrines were articulated. By the time I arrived on the scene, seemingly everything was worth fighting for. Even the smallest biblical point was magnified to rival the virgin birth of Christ in seriousness. Looking back now, it was significantly harder to get into that church than into heaven. I spent my spiritually formative years wondering if I measured up.

As I came into adulthood, and into my first ministry, I experienced another form of complication, the "program model" of ministry. My first pastorate was in a hyperactive church. This church, though in a rural setting, had weekly services Sunday mornings, Sunday nights, and Wednesday nights, an age-graded Sunday school from the cradle to the grave, weekly youth meetings, a midweek children's club program, several choirs and music groups, three banquets each year, an annual missions conference, an annual revival, weekly men's and women's meetings, monthly deacons' meetings, quarterly and annual congregational meetings, and two annual retreats.

How did the church do all this? The answer was another layer of complication. The church had been in existence for forty years and had collected quite an assortment of committees. There was the kitchen committee, the benevolence committee, the missions committee, the men's ministry committee—over thirty committees in all! Just managing these committees was a full-time job. Needless to say, most of everyone's energy went into supporting and maintaining the organizational infrastructure. Complication is the bane of a large organization. Many churches today are overfeatured and unnecessarily complex. The complexity is strangling their ability to grow.

What examples of complication have you observed in the church?

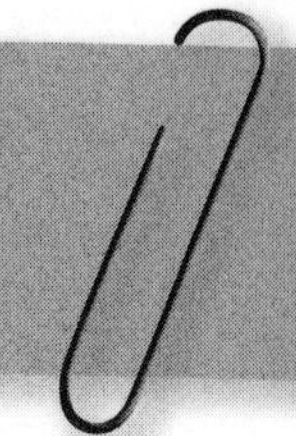

Each epoch of church history has introduced its own layers of complexity. The medieval church introduced hierarchical control, the reformed church introduced theological correctness, the corporate church introduced programmatic complexity. It doesn't really matter how we got here. We got here. To the extent that today's church has become political, institutional, or programmatic, we are making it more complicated than it needs to be.

SIMPLE DELIBERATELY

Complexity causes people to yearn for simple, profound ideas that can be readily related to diverse situations. Deliberate Simplicity delivers these ideas to the church.

We are not espousing simplicity because we haven't yet figured out how to be complicated. We are simple by design. We believe that simplicity is a preferable way to go about things. That's not to say that simplicity is necessarily an easier way to go about things. Simplicity requires a lot of prayer, thought, hard work, and discipline. The paradox of simplicity has been called Meyer's Law: It is a simple task to make things complex, but a complex task to make them simple.

Think about the things in your life that you enjoy because of their simplicity. I think of my Honda Civic, for instance. Why isn't everything designed to be this simple? The answer is, because it's easier to be complicated than it is to be simple. Simple takes much more time and attention. Anybody can be complicated, but simplicity is a gift.

> 'Tis a gift to be simple.
> 'Tis a gift to be free.
> 'Tis a gift to come down where we ought
> to be.
>
> —Shaker Hymn

Bob Buford has achieved success in business and ministry. When he mentors young leaders, he often asks, "What is it that you intentionally do *not* do that fuels your success?" The concept is pretty simple but by no means obvious. As Jim Collins points out in his book *Good to Great*, "Most of us lead busy but undisciplined lives. We have ever-expanding 'to do' lists, trying to build momentum by doing, doing, doing—and doing more. And it rarely works. Those who built the good-to-great companies, however, made as much use of 'stop doing' lists as 'to do' lists. They displayed a remarkable discipline to unplug all sorts of extraneous junk." That's the clarion call of Deliberate Simplicity: to unplug the extraneous.

As Al Ries discusses in his book *Focal Point*, there are only four different things you can do to improve the quality of your life and work:

1. You can do *more* of certain things. You can do more of the things that are of greater value to you and bring you greater rewards and satisfaction.
2. You can do *less* of certain things. You can deliberately decide to reduce activities or behaviors that are not as helpful as other activities.
3. You can *start* to do things you are not doing at all today. You can make new choices, learn new skills, begin new projects or activities, or change the entire focus of your work or personal life.
4. You can *stop* doing certain things altogether. You can stand back and evaluate your life with new eyes. You can then decide to discontinue activities and behaviors that are no longer consistent with what you want and where you want to go.

Which of these four choices is most difficult? Which is least difficult?

While the traditional church tends to choose doors 1 and 3, the Deliberately Simple church looks at what is behind doors 2 and 4. By doing less of certain things, and stopping other things altogether, energy and resources can be reinvested in the few things really worth doing. By not being so broad, we can go deeper.

The mascot for Deliberate Simplicity is the paper clip. The paper clip provides maximum functionality from minimal means. The first bent-wire paper clip was patented by Samuel B. Fay in 1867. It was originally intended primarily for attaching tickets to fabric, although the patent recognized that it could be used to attach paper items together.

Now every year 10,000 tons of steel go into making paper clips. A few years back, during a slowdown in the economy, Lloyd's Bank of London decided to find out what happens to all these paper clips. Lloyd's tracked a batch of 100,000 paper clips within its bank. Here is what they found: 25,000 were simply lost in the shuffle, swept up or vacuumed into oblivion; 19,413 served as card game chips; 14,163 were twisted and made useless during phone conversations; 7,200 were used as hooks for belts, suspenders, or bras; 5,434 were used to pick teeth or scratch ears; 5,308 were used as nail cleaners; 3,196 were used as pipe cleaners. The remaining 20,286, or about 20 percent, were used for their intended purpose of clipping papers together.

Just because something is designed to be simple doesn't mean it will fulfill its intended purpose. This is why we have to be deliberate.

SIMPLIFY

Before Steve Mason agreed to pastor County Christian Center in Laurel, Washington, he had a few stipulations. He made the group of fifty adults commit that the church would focus its energies on three things, and three things only. He asked them to agree that the church would focus on

1. worship
2. small groups
3. outreach

Perhaps out of desperation, the people agreed. Steve wrote up the agreement and had everyone sign it. He moved to Laurel in 1989 to begin his ministry around these three things, and the rest, as they say, is history. County Christian Center would later change its name to Christ the King Community Church, but it never changed its commitment to those three priorities.

Early on, as Steve tells it, those priorities were tested. Various people approached him to ask if the church could get involved in other projects, have other points of emphasis, or initiate other programs. Some were wistful, wishing that the church would reinvent its past. But for the first year Steve did something very strategic: he carried in his pocket the church's written agreement. When discussion would come up about other programs or ministries, Steve would slowly pull the paper out of his pocket and say, "No, these are the things that we agreed upon, worship, small groups, and outreach." The paper in the pocket was an early expression of Deliberate Simplicity that set a course for what CTK would later become.

Many how-to books for church leaders suggest things for the leaders to do (in addition to what they're already doing) to improve the effectiveness of their church. Unfortunately, many pastors are already experiencing diminishing returns (or burnout) from attempting too much. They are trapped in an old paradigm that says, "The only way to increase your productivity is to work harder or longer." But pastors know intuitively that adding more to the list only accelerates their fatigue and demise. Only "super pastors" with extraordinary capacity for administration flourish in such a system. The Clark Kent pastors are burdened, if not overwhelmed, by the complexity. Many are working to the point of exhaustion in an attempt to keep up.

Church participants are also burdened by complexity. The time requirements for many church programs are intense. Added to family, work, and school obligations, the demands can seem unrealistic. Some have even told me they had quit going to church because they didn't have the time. Something is wrong with this picture, and it's not with the people. It's with the system the people are in. As Pastor Wade Hodges opines, "If becoming a part of a church places people in an environment that encourages them to live more frenetic lives than they were living before, then we are going about doing church the wrong way."

Church researcher Kennon Callahan reports,

> People in our time bring with them to congregations the search for help, hope, and home. They are already busy

> and bustling enough in their everyday, ordinary lives. They neither need nor want the mixed blessing of a church that now invites them to be even more busy and bustling than they already are.... People are not looking for a congregation that is trying to do too much too soon. They intuitively know that such a congregation only contributes to their trying to do too much too soon in their own lives. They look for a healthier future than that. People are not looking for a congregation that is going to be something for everyone. Most of us have tried to be something for everyone and have discovered that it does not work. People have the wisdom to know that it does not work for congregations either.[4]

When Callahan says that people are searching for help, hope, and home, is he missing anything?

Deliberate Simplicity advocates restricting the activities of the church instead of expanding them. It calls for less programming instead of more ... working smarter instead of harder. It says, "It's not about the hours you put in; it's about what you put into those hours." It calls us to move the fulcrum so the same (or less) energy is leveraged for greater results. Minimality is how less turns out to be more.

> **min•i•mal** *adj*: smallest possible in amount or least in extent

A friend of mine owns a steel fabrication company with his father. The shop next to theirs has a machine that cuts steel with a jet of water! Powerfully pressurized. Intensely focused. But still just plain ol' H_2O. It is amazing what common elements can do when they are focused well. In a Deliberately Simple church, "deliberate" is the pressure in the hose. "Simple" is what brings powerful definition to the flow.

The elements that compose Christ the King Community Church are really quite common. For instance, we have an emphasis on small groups. This is not new with us. Christians have met in small groups since the first century. We did not invent the small group concept. But we have clarified that this is how we're going to do it. We've made small groups a point of emphasis and accountability. It's the focus of Deliberate Simplicity that gives it power. In his book *Selling the Invisible*, Howard Beckwith writes, "In our increasingly complex world, nothing works more powerfully than simplicity."

Focusing is about making choices, and that means deciding what to leave out as well as what to leave in. As Howard Hendricks says, "The secret of concentration is elimination." Eric Garland puts it this way: "The real work isn't acquisition. It's good, reliable filtering." The development of the immensely popular BlackBerry wireless device by Research In Motion (RIM) is a good illustration.

> Building the BlackBerry meant rejecting some of the computing world's most basic tenets. Even today, no one at RIM would argue that wireless devices are about to eclipse the personal computer. But RIM's employees know from hard-won experience that PC strategies can't compete in a post-PC world.
>
> A case in point: the computer industry's addiction to Moore's Law, the proposition that the number of transistors on a computer chip doubles every 18 months or so. The inevitable result of ever-increasing hardware power is that software writers feel comfortable developing ever-more-complex code—and that's not always a good thing. "In the PC world, you have less engineering discipline

> on the application end, because you know that next year you'll have more memory, a faster processor, and an infinite power supply," says Lazardis. "In wireless, you can't get away with that. Wireless is inherently constrained in terms of memory, power and bandwidth. We develop from scarcity, so we have to be disciplined."
>
> Right from the start, Lazardis believed that what would matter most to the BlackBerry's long-term success was not what RIM put into the device but what it left out. Only by eliminating certain features could engineers extend the life of its power source—a single AAA battery—to three weeks. Only by leaving stuff out could they successfully launch an email message from a two-watt transmitter.[5]

Like RIM, other companies, such as Apple, are finding that less can be more. Why do the users of the iPod enjoy the experience? According to Jonathan Ivie, the VP for Industrial Design, "It's all about removing the unnecessary."

Do you think the limitations of a wireless device are an appropriate analogy for the church? Why or why not?

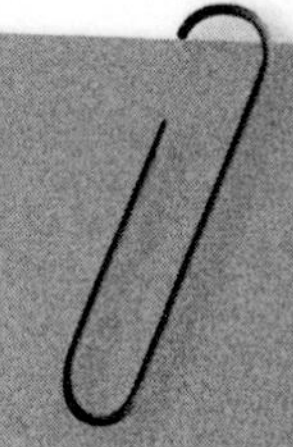

Does the development of a handheld device have application to the church? At first I thought no, because my mind ran immediately to God as our power source. He is infinitely powerful. But on further reflection, I realized that while it does not have application to God, it does have application to *us*. We are finite. We have a limited amount of time and energy. In a sense, we are trying to achieve a high calling on a triple-A battery. We need the discipline of intelligent loss to achieve our purpose. We need to keep asking, "What is the simplest thing that could possibly work?" and jettison other elements even if they have traditionally been associated with progress.

The feature-list wars are not good for technology or church ministry. While adding features gives a list more boxes to check, the features create bulk and may even cloud the real needs of the consumer. What Christians really need is just a simple set of beliefs and practices.

DOCTRINAL MINIMALISTS

As a Deliberately Simple church, we are focused on a core set of beliefs instead of debating theological minutiae and denominational distinctives. We are doctrinal minimalists, in the tradition of Augustine, who said, "In essential matters, unity. In nonessential matters, diversity. In all matters, charity."

People from every conceivable church background—Anglican, Assembly of God, Baptist, Brethren, Calvary Chapel, Catholic, Christian Reformed, Covenant, Episcopalian, Evangelical Free, Foursquare, Lutheran, Methodist, Mennonite, Nazarene, Presbyterian, Reformed, Vineyard—have found a home at Christ the King. One of the reasons why CTK can be common ground for people from so many different backgrounds is that we are doctrinal minimalists. Our degree of dogmatism rises and falls with the degree of clarity in Scripture. Where there is more clarity in Scripture, we are more dogmatic. Where there is less clarity in Scripture, we are less dogmatic. We have found that what unites us is far more important than what divides us. In the words of Clay Crosse, "It all comes down to a man dying on a cross, saving the world."

Major on the Majors

At CTK we have determined that the essential matters are summarized in these four statements:

1. God and his Word are trustworthy.
2. Christ is the Savior and King.
3. There is hope for the future and forgiveness for the past.
4. The church holds the hope of the world in its hands.

First-century Christianity was simple and uncluttered. Early Christian teaching cut through the complexities of culture and allowed what is primary and essential to surface. Like the early church fathers, I am convinced that while there are many things to know, there are not many things you *need* to know to be a fully devoted follower of Christ.

How do you feel after reading the preceding two paragraphs?

I realize that the previous statement may be a hard one to read, so let me clarify. When I say that there are not many things we need to know to be a follower of Christ, I do not mean that we should pick and choose what we believe. I mean that we should pick and choose what we emphasize. We have to get back to basics. While all Scripture is God-breathed and profitable, it is not *equally* profitable. Some Scripture is informative; some is transformative. Some Scripture is interesting; some is life-altering. At CTK we have chosen to focus on the truths that are life-giving and life-changing.

In a Deliberately Simple church, we do not attempt to answer every question out there, just the major ones with eternal implications. We major on the majors and minor on the minors. We stay focused on first-tier beliefs. We try to keep the main thing the main thing. This focus is one of the reasons why the Deliberately Simple church can make such a big impact.

Simply Follow Christ

It is in the area of spiritual formation (some might call it discipleship) that we find out just how complicated we're going to make things. What do Christians need to know to be fully devoted followers of Christ? The answer in a Deliberately Simple church is, not as much as you might think.

New believers can learn enough in just a few days to keep them growing for the rest of their lives. If you are taught to read the Word, pray, be in community, and reach out to others, you have the basic equipment to make the journey.

Even leaders need only minimal indoctrination, if you follow the pattern of the early church. In the New Testament era, the apostle Paul would go into a pagan community, preach Christ, then appoint elders from among the converts before moving on to a new community. He would stay in contact through letters (some of which are in our New Testament), but evidently the basic information needed for leadership in the first-century church could be conveyed in a short period of time.

How was this possible? Obviously, discipleship was defined as a relationship instead of a program. *Disciple* simply means "follower." To say that you are a disciple of Christ is to say, "I'm following him." Once you get pointed in the right direction, time is on your side.

Discipleship in North America has been complicated by the American educational system, an extensive scheme of levels, departments, courses, and grades (101, 201, etc.). Because of this, our inclination is to ask, "Have they taken the course?" The system Christ employed was more relational than informational. Jesus said, "Follow me." That's it. Being a Christ-one is as simple as saying yes to Christ. As Mary stated at the wedding in Cana, "Whatever he tells you to do, do it."

The greatest challenge in discipleship is implementation rather than information. In the area of prayer, for instance, I have not yet become the praying person I want to be, but not for lack of information. I've known for years that prayer is powerful and how to do it. I've just not prayed. In a Deliberately Simple church, we are convinced that the gap holding back most believers is not the gap between what they know and what they don't know. It's the gap between what they know and what they're living. Many Christians are trafficking in unlived truth. They are educated beyond their obedience. The emphasis in a Deliberately Simple church is on living up to what we know.

PRACTICAL MINIMALISTS

With Deliberate Simplicity, we are trying to keep it simple not only in doctrine but in practice. We continually reduce and eliminate activities that take up too much time and contribute very little. We keep going back to basics. By sharpening its focus, the Deliberately Simple church helps the believer concentrate on being a Christ-one.

Prioritize What's Important

Less turns out to be more when elements are well focused. At CTK we have chosen to forego meetings, bazaars, programs, fairs, potlucks, conferences, and other activities typically associated with church so we can have more energy available to put into our priorities: worship, small groups, and outreach.

Tom Peters is a popular business speaker, and he is often asked, "Is it possible to have it all?" Peters responds, "No." He does not believe it is possible to have a fully satisfying personal life and a fully involved work life. He says if you give yourself fully to your career, it's going to cost you: family vacations, Little League games, movies, gardening, etc. One thing will suffer at the expense of the other. Priorities imply that you have to make choices. Some things have to come before other things.

Sometimes priorities compete. For this reason it is often helpful to rank them. For instance, at Disneyland one of their priorities is the show (as in "the show must go on"). Employees dressed in character are to remain in character at all times. Another priority for Disneyland is safety. But safety is ranked as a higher priority than the show. So if an employee were to see a child endangered on a ride, she would know that she should take off her costume, if necessary, to rescue the child.

Think of a scenario in which a church's priorities might come into conflict with each other. How would their ranking resolve the conflict?

The priorities of a Deliberately Simple church are also ranked in order: worship, small groups, and outreach. We are devoted to worshiping God as a lifestyle. We are determined to care for each other through small groups. We are dedicated to reaching people who do not know Christ. While these priorities rarely conflict, if they do, we know that our first priority is the worship of God, our second is convening people in small groups, and our third is outreach. You might say that as we worship God, we want to gather together and reach out. Worship is the way we stay centered. Small groups is the way we stay connected. Outreach is the way we stay concerned.

Do What Works

In his book *Managing in a Time of Great Change*, Peter Drucker asserts that groups fail because "in most cases, the right things are being done—but fruitlessly ... the assumptions on which the organization has been built and is being run no longer fit reality."

When Drucker says the right things are being done, he means according to the written and unwritten rules of the organization.

Maybe a church has a certain way it's going about things, and it's the way the church is "supposed" to be going about things (maybe because "we've always done it this way"). But it's not working. It's the difference between efficiency and effectiveness. Efficiency is doing things right. Effectiveness is doing the right things. The key word when dealing with things is *efficiency*. The key word when dealing with people is *effectiveness*. A Deliberately Simple church takes limited resources (time, money, energy) and streamlines its offerings for effectiveness.

Has the traditional church given more focus to efficiency or effectiveness? How can you tell?

Being strategic means having a carefully devised plan of action to achieve a goal. When I coached one of my kids' teams, I told the kids to remember three things as they went out to play: (1) have fun, (2) do your best, and (3) try to win. It is that third component that often separates the deliberate church from the traditional church. We try to win. We are attempting to be as strategic as we possibly can with our efforts.

Everyone who has a goal in mind sits down and tries to come up with a way to win. This is true in sports (there's a game plan), in business (there's a business plan), in war (there's a battle plan). Where it is often not true is in the church. We have the most important mission on planet earth, but we aren't very strategic in carrying it out. We try to please everyone except our Commander in Chief. We need to plan our work and work our plan.

Churches may take different approaches. But every church needs to grapple with how to do what Jesus told us to do in the

Great Commission: to make more disciples of Jesus Christ. It's not enough to have a mission statement (that's a good first step). We need a spirit-inspired, strategic game plan to make it work.

At CTK we have chosen small groups as our Plan A (and there is no Plan B). CTK is not a church with small groups. It's a church of small groups. Small groups are not just another program. They are our essential and nearly exclusive activity. While most churches are organized by hundreds in hopes of reaching thousands, we are organized by tens in hopes of reaching tens of thousands.

Small groups are our basic building block, and the primary way that we care for people. In addition to being scriptural (house to house), small groups are strategic. They put people into the ministry (every person in a group has a ministry to every other person in the group). They position people for outreach (every group is a lifeboat praying over the empty chair). They offer many entry points for new people (dozens of side doors into the church in addition to the front door). They assimilate people rapidly (it should be difficult for people to "just attend" a small group church). They enhance retention (it is harder to leave when you know you will be missed). They facilitate a manageable span of care (everyone's needs are met). They provide a forum for leadership development (you need at least one leader for every ten people). They are simple (no production crew or equipment required). They are satisfying (they put you in touch with the eternal). They are scalable (you can have as many small groups as you have leaders and living rooms). They are successful (the first-century church spread rapidly house to house).

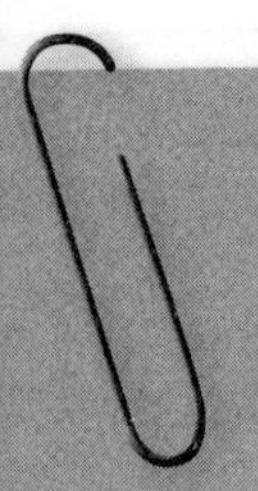

From the preceding paragraph, which three qualities of small groups do you particularly appreciate?

In San Francisco, pollsters took a survey and asked, "What do Christians do?" They received two primary answers: "They go to a lot of meetings" and "They are against things." Obviously, the culture around us is missing the essence of Christ's message. Partly why I believe the Deliberately Simple church works is that the priorities of worship, small groups, and outreach express directly Jesus' great commandments to love God and to love people.

Worship	Love God more
Small Groups	Love people more
Outreach	Love more people

G. K. Chesterton was a maverick Christian thinker and writer in the early 1900s. In his day it had become widely accepted not to discuss religion or politics. So, just to buck the system, for thirty years he wrote a column about religion and politics. His biographer, Dale Ahlquist, affirmed his decision. "If you think about it, every controversy, every argument, every discussion is really about religion or politics. Or both. Religion has to do with our relationship with God. Politics has to do with our relationship with our neighbor. These are controversial for the simple reason that all the problems in the world come from our failure to obey the two great commandments: to love God and to love our neighbor."

Deliberate Simplicity attempts to fulfill the Great Commission by fulfilling the great commandments. Because we want to love God well, we have deliberately chosen to be a worshiping church. And because we want to love people well, we have chosen to gather in small groups to put feet to our prayers.

A Deliberately Simple church is focused on doing a few things and doing those few things well. I regularly repeat to the folks at CTK, "We're here to learn how to love God and people well. Once we get that down, we'll move on to other things." Outside of small group meetings and worship services, we initiate few programs. And those programs that are initiated are usually organized into small groups and then critically evaluated for effectiveness. If they don't help us love God and people better, they don't continue. It's the art of abandoning. It's not particularly easy, but it's pretty simple.

How difficult do you think it is to initiate few programs? How about critically evaluating programs for effectiveness? Which is tougher, in your opinion?

SMALL IS HUGE

Hitting the Small Time

In a Deliberately Simple church, smallness is valued. Because of this there are opportunities available to the Deliberately Simple church that are precluded from the traditional church, where "bigger and better" outline the thinking.

For instance, Christ the King Community Church has experienced a decided advantage by starting in smaller urban communities. Typically, in smaller towns and burgs there is no megachurch, because there is not the population (or money) to support it. There are often a few ingrown traditional churches. In that context, a church willing to keep the main thing the main thing and do a few things well can make a significant impact.

In his fascinating book *The Innovator's Dilemma*, Clayton M. Christenson chronicles the fall of major industry leaders to disruptive technologies. A disruptive technology is typically simpler, cheaper, more reliable, and more convenient than established technologies. For years Seagate was the leader in hard disk drives, building hard drives that were bigger and faster than previous models. They were so fixated on serving the desktop computer market that they missed the emerging laptop and palmtop markets, where smallness was valued. PDAs heralded a change in the basis of competition. The rules of the game switched to smaller drives with less capacity, but Seagate was not ready for it. The competition came in under them, where there was a lot of room to roam, and soon toppled Seagate's dominance. Leading companies in other industries—from construction equipment to pharmaceuticals—have also overshot the functionality required by the market and have lost out to nimble upstarts.

Small is the new big. There is a sea change from "bigger is better" to "smaller is sweeter" in manufacturing, retailing, and media. For example:

The Boeing Company was faced with a strategic decision when contemplating the next generation of airplane beyond the 767. Airbus, their European rival, decided to go bigger and develop a superjumbo jet—an aircraft that makes the 747 look little. Boeing decided to take the other direction and develop a highly economical but smaller "Dreamliner." It appears that the Dreamliner will be first to market. Production complications with the Airbus megajet have caused top executives to be fired and Airbus to stall. Meanwhile, Chicago-based Boeing is on track to deliver its deliberately simple jet, and for the first time in many years has surpassed Airbus in orders and deliveries. It's not that the Airbus jet won't find a place in the market, but Boeing seems to have tapped into the prevailing trend of direct, smaller, point-to-point air carrier routes. Airbus is hemmed in by the old hub-and-spoke model of air travel.

Two new game systems were released in November 2006: Nintendo's Wii and Sony's PlayStation 3. Both systems found gamers camping out overnight to be first in line. But only the Nintendo system has had extended demand issues. This in spite of the fact (maybe because of the fact) that Sony's is feature rich (high definition, Blu-ray DVD, blah blah blah), with a price point of $600. In contrast, Nintendo's offering was deliberately simple, with a price point of $250. Courageously, Nintendo decided to make its Wii unit play back in standard definition, not high definition, arguing that "it's the games that truly matter." It did, however, add a participatory feature: there are two handsets, one for each hand, that allow the player to interact with the characters on screen (box with both hands, etc.). Needless to say, it is the less-sophisticated Wii that has won over the highly cynical gaming community, not the over-the-top PlayStation 3.

Two guys in a bedroom with a webcam created a dramatic series for YouTube that has confounded the major TV networks: lonelygirl15. There is only one on-screen character, an actress named Jessica Rose. Each episode is two minutes long and chronicles the life of a suburban teen as she discusses her relationships. Some episodes have had as many as one million viewers (successful TV sitcoms have between three hundred thousand and five hundred thousand). Cost to produce? Paltry in comparison with major network productions. And *Wired* magazine contributing editor Joshua Davis says that simplicity is actually preferable for this new medium of internet video: "It doesn't need to be lit like a film—that would make it feel less real. The camera work should be simple. There shouldn't be a disembodied third-person camera—a character is always filming the action. Each episode needs to be short, no more than three minutes." This is not your father's television.

I was going to say, "There's a new day coming," but it might be more accurate to say, "It's already here." The movement from big to small, from centralized to decentralized, and from passive to participatory has reached us. And by "us" I mean "us, the church." Small is going to be the new big in the church too. The church has generally followed society in its belief that bigger is better. If a church of one hundred is good, one thousand is better, and ten thousand is best. As George Barna says, "We are more impressed by a church of 4000 people who have no clue about God's character and His expectations, than by a church of 100 deeply committed saints who are serving humankind in quiet but significant ways." Because of this mental model, church planters tend to do extensive demographic studies before planting a new church, to ensure there is sufficient population density. Herein lies a tremendous disruptive opportunity for the Deliberately Simple church. We can see the beauty in smallness.

Living Large in Small Places

Extra-large is not as popular a size in our culture as it used to be. For instance, there is a trend in home buying away from larger and larger homes to smaller, cozier dwellings. A bigger house does not make a better one. *Cottage* is the feel-good word of the new millennium. *USA Today* columnist Craig Wilson reports, "Though most Americans don't live in cottages, the term is being used to connote an informality that can be translated to any style of architecture.... The idea is to offer a more lived-in look. Kids jumping on beds. The man of the house reclining on the sofa." People are finding that small spaces can still give you a big feeling, and that it is the quality and character of the space rather than the size of it that matters. Consider this article from the May 16, 2003, edition of *USA Today*, titled "McMansion Passion Is Diminishing":

> Home buyers who once hungered for supersized domiciles might be losing their appetites, say some trend analysts and home design professionals. The ready-made mansions are still marching on suburbia, but some move-up buyers are rejecting them in favor of scaled-down homes with features tailored to their personal tastes, says architect and author Sarah Susanka in Raleigh, N.C.
>
> "Many people are reassessing whether it makes sense to buy a massive house to gain volumes of space, half of which will go unused," says Susanka, whose books, including

The Not So Big House, promote a scaled-down school of thought. "Comfort," she says, "is born of smaller scale and fine details."[6]

This is a significant shift in direction for the housing market, as home sizes have steadily increased for decades. The average house in the 1950s was 900 square feet, and often built without a garage. In the 1970s that average house was 1,400 square feet, with a double garage. The average home today is 2,300 square feet, with a triple garage becoming the new standard (licensed cars in the United States now exceed the number of licensed drivers). When is enough enough? That is the question for flourishing consumers as well as program-glutted churches.

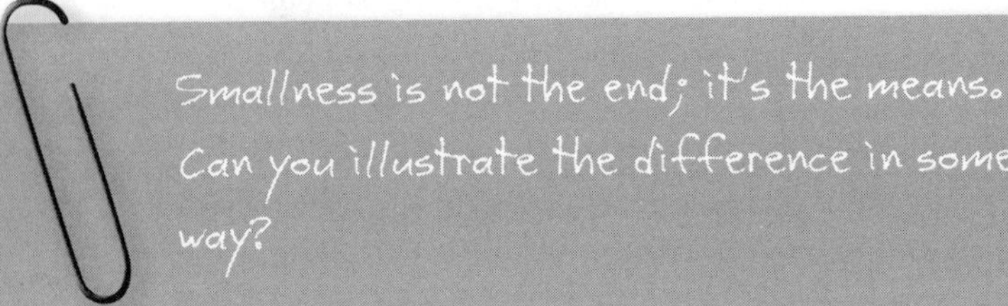

Civic officials are also starting to take a more tapered approach. Traffic engineer Hans Monderman says, "The trouble with traffic engineers is that when there's a problem with a road, they always try to add something. To my mind, it's better to remove things." Monderman is a proponent of removing signs and curbs to improve safety. (One study even suggested removing center lines, observing that drivers with no center line to guide them drove more safely and had a 35 percent decrease in the number of accidents.) New Jersey's Department of Transportation has taken note and is now moving away from congested freeways strewn with malls toward a series of linked minivillages with narrow roads. It's Deliberate Simplicity applied to city planning.

No Small Wonder

Each fall, my family makes its annual pilgrimage to the county fair. I'm not exactly sure why I let my kids drag me back year after year. Absolutely nothing changes, that I can tell, from one year to the next. I swear I could walk through the fairgrounds blindfolded and point out the rides and attractions. But one thing I do enjoy is watching people.

People are so interesting (they're looking back at me thinking the same thing, I'm sure). One of the moments I captured (or that captured me) was a toddler getting off the merry-go-round. My son Daron and I were standing in line at the entrance gate. This little girl was following her mother out the exit gate. Then she abruptly stopped, went back, and patted one of the horses, saying, "Thank you, horsey." The cynical, adult part of me thought, "Little kids really don't get it, do they?" But then another voice in me said, "Maybe they do."

There is not always a correlation between size and significance. The most important light in your house may be not the chandelier in the dining room but the little night-light that keeps you from stubbing your toe when you get up at night.

The best things in life are really kind of simple. The merry-go-round is one of these attractions. It simply goes up and down and round and round. But it catches you by surprise. Something magical takes place as an outcome far greater than the process. Small groups possess this quality. Jesus said, "Where two or three come together in my name, there am I with them" (Matt. 18:20). We show up in his name. God shows up. God things happen (yes, I spelled that right). Pretty simple really but pretty amazing. And hard to beat.

I was at a Christian rock festival with some young adults one year and had parked my car at the edge of the campsite. Later, when I noticed some kids gathered around my car, I felt a bit ashamed of the "pastoral Civic" (it really is a pretty tame car compared with the Chevy Camaro with a 327 Corvette engine I had at their age). Then one of the young men approached me and asked, "What year is your Civic?" I replied sheepishly, "1995." He said, "Wow, that is a really good year! I would love to have a 1995 Civic!" My chest began to push out with pride as I said, "Yeah, it is a really good year." Sometimes you are surprised that what you have is really more valuable than you thought.

Small groups are more valuable than you think. Christian educator Margaret Mead once instructed, "Never doubt that a small group of thoughtful, committed citizens can change the world.... Indeed, it is the only thing that ever has." To have a place to be heard, to be encouraged, to share, to be loved, to learn about God, to pray for others, and to have others pray for you is no small wonder.

Small but Sacred

After watching the evening news of our messed-up world, a man says to his wife, "I'm going to go get some air." She knows what he means. He is going to go for a walk with the dog while she does the dishes. And as he walks, he will process the affairs of the day. He will notice nature again. He will breathe deeply. He will find peace. Each evening, he performs a ritual act of *sacer simplicitus*: "sacred simplicity." It is a small thing, but it is huge. It has a disproportionate impact on his spiritual health and renewal.

Deliberate Simplicity is always on the lookout for these moments of disproportionate impact. There is a "Law of Exchange" at work on all our relationships. I'm not saying that this is good or bad, just that it is. The law says that every human interaction is an exchange, or a trade. The goal is to make good exchanges. This law also applies to a person's relationship with God. When someone prays or reads the Bible, they are making an exchange. They are exchanging their time for what will hopefully be worth more than their time: an encounter with God.

At Christ the King we advocate ten plus ten—ten minutes a day in prayer, and ten minutes a day in the Word. Some may spend more than that, but we ask everyone at CTK to spend a minimum of twenty minutes per day interacting with God. There are a lot of other things we could do that won't make the impact that daily time with God will. It's a great exchange.

When someone is recruited into ministry, an exchange is taking place. You are asking the person to give up freedoms, but in exchange for what? There could be many answers, including (a) an opportunity to be in close community with others, (b) a chance to "get in the game," (c) the reward of making a contribution to something eternal, etc. But the highest and best payoff is closeness with God.

Intimate small groups and impacting worship services—the basic activities of a Deliberately Simple church—are both worthwhile exchanges because they possess *sacer simplicitus*. It is inherently edifying to experience the community of a small group or the celebration of corporate worship. It doesn't take something out of you; it puts something in you. There is disproportional return on investment.

GOOD ENOUGH IS GOOD ENOUGH

In the 1970s Tom Peters burst onto the scene as a business guru with a groundbreaking book entitled *In Search of Excellence*. The excellence emphasis has dominated organizational thought for the past thirty years. Now Tom says to seminar audiences that he will not hire a person with a 4.0 grade point average. He's not against intelligence; he just feels that a 4.0 is an indicator that the person has not been playing enough. There may not be balance there. Perhaps it's time for a new treatise, *In Search of Good Enough*.

Deliberate Simplicity advocates good enough instead of excellence. I know this sounds like heresy in the face of the "excellence honors God and inspires people" dogma of many traditional megachurches. And I used to be fanatical about excellence myself. I'm not against it now, but I've come to realize that too much of a good thing can be just as unsatisfactory as too little of it. Happy ends up being somewhere between not enough and too much.

The Comfort Zone

The balanced approach Deliberate Simplicity takes can be illustrated by the thermostat dial I remember on the wall in my childhood home. The thermostat had a shaded area on it about two-thirds of the way around the radius, marked "comfort zone."

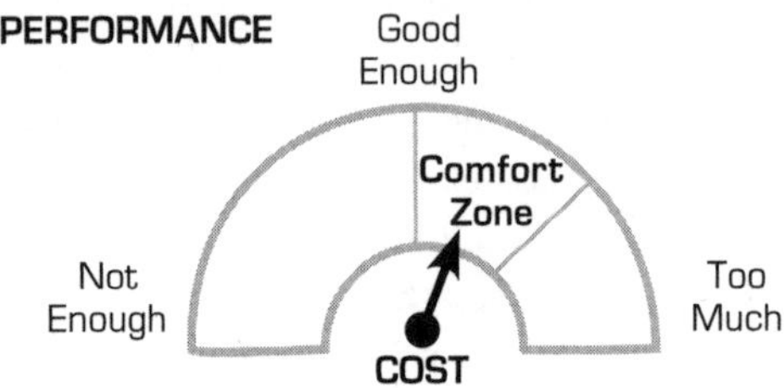

The inner and outer radius of the dial represent cost and performance. At the left side of the dial is less cost and performance. At the right side is greater cost and performance. The comfort zone has a bottom and top edge that represent a reasonable balance. Set the dial below the comfort zone, and house temperatures might be uncomfortably cool. Above the comfort zone, the temperature might be needlessly warm and inordinately costly.

Christian Schwarz, in *Natural Church Development*, explores the bottom edge of the comfort zone, describing "the minimum factor." Schwartz uses a wooden barrel with vertical staves of varying lengths to illustrate that the level of impact for a church will not exceed its lowest stave. Truly, ministries are ineffective when they do not reach a minimal level of performance in essential areas. Just as true, however, is that churches can overfunction. Deliberate Simplicity explores the top edge of the comfort zone and suggests that there are diminishing returns beyond good enough.

> You may have heard it said, "If it can't be done with excellence, don't do it." Well, Jesus never said that! The truth is, almost everything we do is done poorly when we first start doing it—that's how we learn. At Saddleback Church, we

> practice the "good enough" principle: It doesn't have to be perfect for God to use and bless it. We would rather involve thousands of regular folks in ministry than have a perfect church run by a few elites.
>
> —Rick Warren, *The Purpose Driven Church*

Jesus not only did not stress excellence; he actually encouraged planned neglect, at least with Martha. When her work got in the way of her worship, she was rebuked. Sometimes trying harder is nothing more than preventing God from working more. Sometimes an emphasis on excellence is just a product of unhealthy perfectionism. Sometimes it's evidence of a lack of faith that God can feed thousands with only five loaves and two fishes. Sometimes it stems from an unhealthy need to control (things being a lot easier to control than people). In any case, God is not into extremism. He wants his kingdom to expand, but in a healthy, balanced way.

Good enough is called good enough because it's good enough. The fact that you probably have an ink-jet printer instead of a laser printer validates this hypothesis. An ink-jet printer is slower than a laser printer, its resolution is worse, and its cost per printed page is higher. But the printer itself is smaller and less expensive than a laser printer. And the critical question is not whether an ink-jet printer is as good as it can possibly be but whether it's as good as you actually need.

> In their history, Band-Aids have probably allowed millions of people to keep working or playing tennis or cooking or walking when they would otherwise have had to stop. The Band-Aid solution is actually the best kind of solution because it involves solving a problem with the minimum amount of effort and time and cost. We have, of course, an instinctive disdain for this kind of solution because there is something in all of us that feels that true answers have to be comprehensive.... There are times when we need a convenient shortcut, a way to make a lot out of a little.
>
> —Malcolm Gladwell, *The Tipping Point*

One area in which good enough has served CTK well is the area of music. Hundreds of musicians lead worship across the CTK network. Their musicianship ranges from average to extraordinary. Yet worship is consistently considered a strong suit for CTK. By keeping the expectations reasonable, we have been able to engage a large number of musicians and keep the awe and wonder where it belongs, on Christ.

One megachurch in the Midwest had turned the temperature up to such a degree in the area of music that, when they launched a new church location, they were held up because they could not find a worship leader who was talented enough. Mind you, this was in a city the size of Chicago, in a church the size of many small towns. They ended up videotaping their worship experience and playing it at their new site until they finally were able to recruit the lead singer of a well-known Christian rock band. Evidently, their paradigm required them to find someone in the 99th percentile.

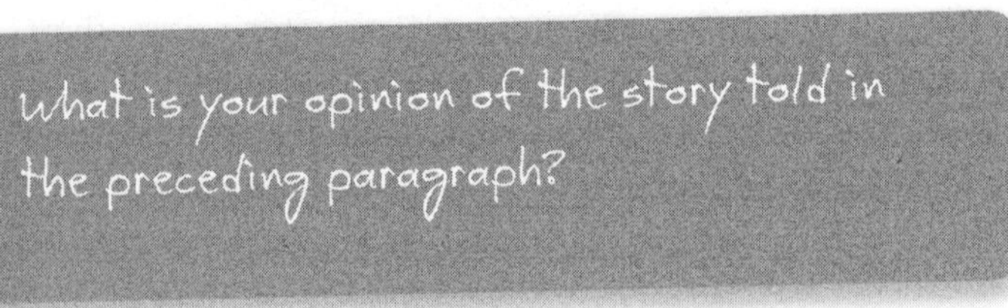

In a Deliberately Simple church, we tend to use the 80th percentile as our rule of thumb. Will the new person be able to execute his or her role at least 80 percent as well as the person being replaced (or the person we would wish for)? If the answer is yes, we move forward, because we find that for most people the difference between 80 percent and 100 percent, in terms of how it impacts their experience, is negligible. It's the difference between a paper printed on an ink-jet printer and a paper printed on a laser printer. The one from the laser printer has higher resolution (if you care to look that closely), but the other is good enough for most applications.

> If you expect people to come to church just to hear your music, you'll be disappointed. If they want to hear music, they'll pop in a CD. It's better quality than you can do. The unchurched will not crawl out of bed ... to watch your drama. They can get a lot better drama on television by watching a rerun of *Seinfeld* or *Friends* or whatever show is hot today. If they want to sit around tables and talk, they'll go to Starbucks.... Present God's Word in a clear, compelling way with a deliberate sensitivity to those you're trying to reach, because the Word of God alone has the power to bring people to Christ and keep them there.
>
> —Ron Gladden, *The Seven Habits of Highly Ineffective Churches*

The web tool RSS (Really Simple Syndication) has been criticized for being limited in its functionality. But its creators have resisted all attempts to elevate RSS to a "higher" level. While it could become more rigorous, it would not be as simple and easy to use. So they are keeping the code deliberately simple. Likewise, I tell teaching pastors in the CTK network, "You don't need to hit a home run in your teaching each weekend. Just try to make contact."

The difference between excellence and good enough is the difference between the production of a full-length movie and the production of the nightly news. Movies are at the top of the quality curve, taking months, if not years, to get it right. The nightly news is at the bottom of the curve, with just hours, if not minutes, to get it on the air. Both have their place, and viewers appreciate their relative qualities. And there's a market for both. Deliberate Simplicity, like the nightly news, stays in the steep part of the curve.

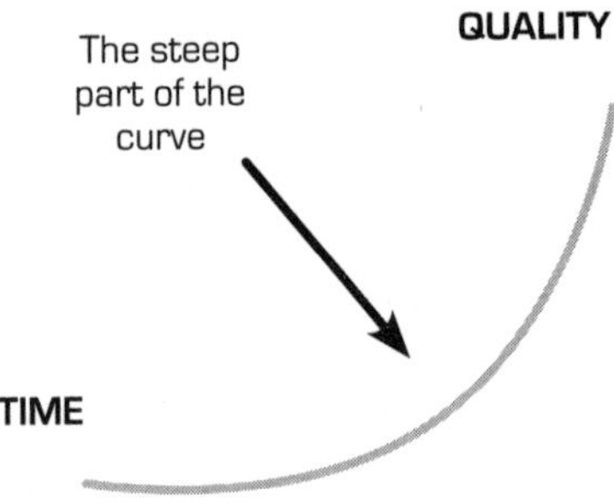

One of my favorite success stories in the steep part of the curve is Burt Rutan's *SpaceShipOne*. Rutan, who has designed over three hundred airplanes, was hired by billionaire Paul Allen to design a spacecraft capable of winning the X Prize—a ten million dollar reward for the first privately produced, manned vehicle to make two trips into outer space. With a staff of twelve, Rutan took off-the-shelf rocket engines and components—the interior handles he got out of a passenger van in a junkyard—and with ingenuity, smart design, and the laws of physics was able to design a spaceship that would go over sixty miles above earth! It was Deliberate Simplicity applied to the space industry. X Prize board member Barry Thompson sees parallels to the computer industry: "The evolution from mainframe machines to the PC is parallel to the shift from the traditional space industry to space tourism. Yes, the X Prize is suborbital. But that's just a baby step, like the first PC. People said there'd never be a market for them and look what happened."

Because of the success of Rutan and his team, there are now two ways to get into outer space—the traditional NASA way, which takes years and costs billions, and the *SpaceShipOne* way, at a tiny fraction of the time, labor, and cost. I'm sure there were NASA engineers who were wagging their fingers and saying, "That's not the way to do that!" ... right up until *SpaceShipOne* returned successfully from its eighty-minute journey to space.

By emphasizing adequate rather than superior functionality, the Deliberately Simple church creates opportunities for average people to go to heights they wouldn't think possible. It's the stuff that movements are made of, as modeled by the QuickBooks craze.

> Intuit, the maker of financial management software, is known primarily for its extraordinarily successful personal financial software package, Quicken. Quicken dominates its market because it is easy and convenient. Its makers pride themselves on the fact that the vast majority of Quicken customers simply buy the program, boot it up on their computers, and begin using it without having to read the instruction manual. Its developers made it so convenient to use, and continue to make it simpler and more convenient, by watching how customers use the product, not by listening to what they or the "experts" say they need. By watching for small hints of where the product might be difficult or confusing to use, the developers direct their energies toward a progressively simpler, more convenient product that provides adequate, rather than superior, functionality.... Intuit's disruptive QuickBooks changed the basis of product competition from functionality to convenience and captured 70 percent of its market within two years of its introduction.
>
> —Clayton M. Christenson, *The Innovator's Dilemma*

Do you think it would be wise for the church in America to consider changing its point of emphasis from functionality to convenience?

Just Enough

A landmark study of California companies found that the cost of innovation, as measured by new products and patents, is an astounding twenty-four times greater at large companies than at small companies. Christian Schwarz reported, in his book *Natural Church Development*, that the evangelistic effectiveness of mini-churches is statistically 1,600 percent greater than that of mega-churches.

In a Deliberately Simple church, we think big but act small. We keep asking, "What is the simplest thing that could possibly work?" We try to have just enough to facilitate our mission. Just enough money. Just enough time. Just enough leaders. Just enough space. Just enough advertising. We don't want to stockpile assets. We want to have everything in motion for the kingdom. Often assets do double duty to maximize return on investment.

Most of the worship centers at CTK have begun with an investment of less than five thousand dollars. Would we like more to work with? Certainly. Do we need more? Evidently not. We've always had everything we've needed.

It is possible to start a Deliberately Simple church with next to nothing. It can be done with a borrowed sound system, a rented community hall, a pastor-on-loan, and a pieced-together worship team. Some denominations claim it costs them up to two million dollars to plant a church. That sounds like Deliberate Complexity to me.

Progress isn't all it's cracked up to be. It costs us more and it promises more, but it doesn't always deliver. I was in a discount department store looking for razor blades, and I noticed that there was a pack of twenty cartridges for five dollars (instead of five cartridges for twenty dollars, like it seems I usually pay). Unfortunately, they wouldn't work on my newer razor (you know, the one designed for four-blade cartridges). These were generic cartridges that fit the old Atra razor (only two measly blades.... how did we ever think we could shave back then?!). I did something courageous that I am now very happy about: I tossed my newer razor and went back to the old Atra (yes, I am now shaving with "only" two blades) and bought the twenty pack. They are working great. And I figure I will save about fifty dollars on razor blades this year. Sometimes progress means going backward.

Is there a parallel to church ministry? I think so. We need to rewind "overfeaturized" churches back to version 1.0. Blake Ross and Ben Goodger have done that with their web browser, Firefox. Frustrated by the glitchiness and insecurity of Microsoft's bulky Internet Explorer, they created a stripped-down version of the old Netscape Navigator's code base, Mozilla. Inspired by Google's simple interface, their goal was modest: no bloat. "Lots of Mozilla people didn't get it," Ross recalls. "They'd say, 'This is just the product we have now, but with less features.' Meanwhile, the Mozilla product at the time had about 10,000 options. You basically needed to know the secret handshake to get anything done. It sounds corny, but it was important to make something that Mom and Dad could use." They did. By the conclusion of the first day that Firefox was available, they had over one million downloads. In the last quarter of 2004, Firefox experienced 54 percent growth in market share in the U.S. browser market. During the same period, Internet Explorer experienced a negative 2 percent growth rate. Firefox is Deliberate Simplicity applied to software development. They are moving forward swiftly by staying lean.

Specialty retailer Trader Joe's simplifies the shopping experience for its customers by offering only one or two choices of each item in its market. This is a help to shoppers who often feel overwhelmed by the overwhelming variety of products on supermarket shelves. In some ways this is a similar strategy to that of Oprah Winfrey's hugely popular book club. Oprah selects a book of the month, which takes the work out of finding a good book to read. People can then get on to the joy of actually reading.

Proponents of minimality are modern-day reformers. A key word for the church will always be *reformation* (literally re-form-ation)—taking the forms of the original church and recasting in those molds.

> All conservatism is based upon the idea that if you leave things alone you leave them as they are. But you do not. If you leave a thing alone you leave it to a torrent of change. If you leave a white fence post alone it will soon be a black post. If you particularly want it to be white you must be always painting it again; that is, you must be always having a revolution. Briefly, if you want the old white post you must have a new white post.
>
> —G. K. Chesterton

Minimality may look like a new white post. It is actually an old white post. The more the church moves into the future, the more it will look like the church of the past.

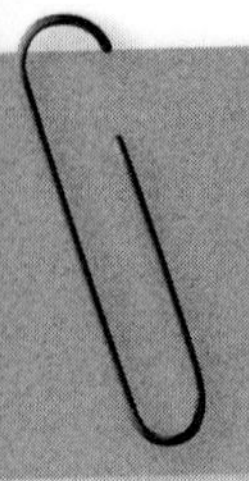

Do you think Chesterton's statement accounts for the decline of the mainline denominations? Explain.

WHAT BUSINESS ARE WE IN?

Deliberate Simplicity is a commitment to high definition — to proceed aggressively in the work of outreach, with "more signal, less noise." By making an up-front investment in unusual clarity, a Deliberately Simple church reaps the benefit of spending less time and energy trying to figure out what it's trying to do and more time doing it. Coherence and consistency are a by-product of clarity.

A vivid illustration of the lack of clarity that exists among Christians came during an organizational meeting I held in a community where we were considering establishing a new Christ the King worship center. After sharing with the group our commitment to reach out to lost people, a well-meaning woman raised her hand and asked, "Isn't the church for those of us who are believers?" A hush fell over the room as everyone awaited my response.... Little did she know she was surfacing one of the most defining precepts of Deliberate Simplicity. The clarity of my response probably startled her. I said, "No, the church is not *for* us. The church *is* us, but it's not *for* us. We are here for the lost."

You cannot do work that matters until you define what matters. A leader's job is to clarify and simplify so everyone understands what's truly important. Peter Drucker says that the two diagnostic questions every organization must answer are, "What business are we in?" and "How's business?" But before you can answer the question, "How's business?" you need to know what business you are in. What is the business of the church? In short, it is to make more disciples of Jesus Christ.

President Calvin Coolidge believed that "no enterprise can exist for itself alone. It ministers to some great need, it performs some great service, not for itself, but for others; or failing therein it ceases to be profitable and ceases to exist." Perhaps that statement summarizes the reason why many churches are sick and dying.

Rick Warren, pastor of Saddleback Community Church and author of *The Purpose Driven Church*, suggests that every church is driven by something. Some of the organizing principles that churches adopt (maybe unknowingly) include:

- *Tradition*. A church driven by tradition finds itself looking to the past for guidance for the future. As an explanation for why things are done (or not done) a certain way, you may hear, "We've always done it that way" or "We've never done it that way." Those in the church soon learn to take special care not to arouse the ghosts of the past.
- *Personality*. A church driven by personality finds itself directed by a key figure or figures. You may hear it said, "We need to talk with so-and-so before we change that." The name that goes in the blank may be not the pastor's but the name of a long-standing member who has, over time, hijacked the power structure. The energy of the organization goes into appeasing this person.
- *Finances*. A church driven by finances finds itself looking at the budget for direction. If it's in the budget, we can do it. If it's not, we can't. The energy in a finance-driven church is spent preparing and lobbying for items to be included or

excluded from the budget and/or raising funds to meet the budget.

- *Programs.* A church driven by programs defines itself by the programs it offers. Program-driven churches take a twist on the bumper sticker that says, "He who dies with the most toys wins," and it is, "The church with the most programs wins." Unfortunately, programs initiated to meet specific needs can soon take on a life of their own, and people can end up serving the programs instead of the programs serving the people. Programs that have outlived their usefulness continue indefinitely with life support. Sacred cows cannot be looked at critically, much less slaughtered. With so many accumulated slots to fill, a constant complaint is that there are not enough people willing to do what needs to be done. In this type of church, a lot of energy is burned up trying to recruit people to fill the holes in church programs.
- *Buildings.* A church driven by buildings finds itself in constant pursuit of bigger and better facilities. It encounters a danger similar to the one faced by program-driven churches — that of the means becoming the end. The church's building, which originally was designed to be a tool for ministry, ends up being the church's identity and the focus for its energies. In a building-driven church, there is usually an architectural drawing on the easel or a capital campaign under way for the next phase.
- *Events.* A church driven by events finds itself regularly gearing up for its next concert or pageant or bazaar. While events can be an effective part of any church's strategy, left unchecked, events can grow to *be* the ministry. Over time, the energy of the church goes into making the next year's event bigger and better, and little energy is left for anything else.
- *Seekers.* A church driven by seekers finds itself trying to get into the mind of "the customer." Surveys are taken. The results are evaluated. The church's ministry is driven by

polling data. The energy of the body goes into being culturally relevant and seeker-friendly.

- *Purpose.* A church driven by purpose finds itself evaluating what it does in relation to its sense of purpose. It has a philosophy of ministry that begins with the question, what is the church supposed to do? The church's goals and objectives become the ruler by which efforts are measured.

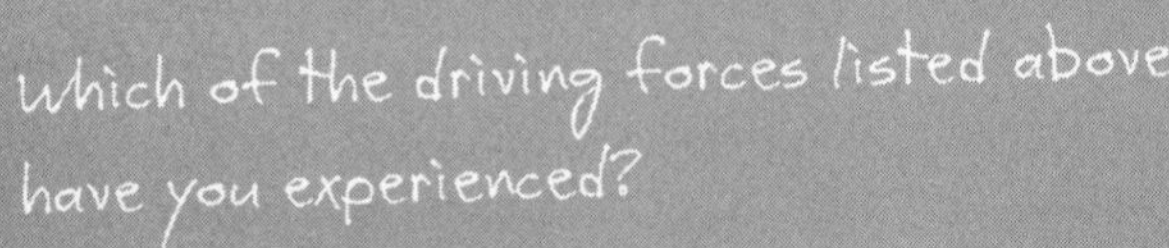

What is the driving force behind a Deliberately Simple church? As the word *deliberate* implies, a Deliberately Simple church is very purposeful in its approach. It is intentional in its strategies and behaviors. But the Deliberately Simple church narrows its impetus to a subset of purpose: mission.

- *Mission.* A church driven by mission is carrying out marching orders from its Commanding Officer. This is *the purpose* for the church's existence. Resources are allocated to fulfill this mandate. The energies of the participants go to carrying out the mission. The mission is the impetus.

At CTK we prefer to be called mission-driven instead of purpose-driven for three reasons. One is that the word *mission* has a greater sense of movement to it. It means we are on the march, advancing. Second, *mission* gives the sense that there is a cause much greater than us. We are engaged in a great enterprise with orders from above. Theoretically, we could come up with a purpose on our own. But a mission is something we have been given. The third reason we call ourselves mission-driven is that the term *purpose-driven* is widely associated with megachurches like Saddleback Community Church. Since we are aspiring to be a minichurch, it makes sense for us not to confuse the issue.

When a church gives a high priority to serving their community, its participants are energized. Leadership guru Warren Bennis says, "All great groups believe they are on a mission from God." People have to live to leave a legacy. The greatest sin of the church today is not any sin of commission or sin of omission but the sin of no mission. David Neeleman, CEO of Jet Blue, recognizes that "there are irrevocable laws of heaven that when you serve others, you get this little buzz."

Shortly after we launched Christ the King Community Church in Skagit Valley, Washington, a man from a neighboring church came to visit one Sunday. In an effort to be complimentary of what we were doing, he said something quite startling. He said, "It's a good thing that you guys are here, because our building is full." Let that statement sink in for a second. Seldom does someone say something so clearly dysfunctional with a smile on his face. Since when is the church's job to fill a building with people? That's not the mission! The mission is to reach the world for Christ. His statement was revealing, however. The average church is not thinking outside the box.

Deliberate Simplicity clearly defines the church's essence as missional. The bottom line is outreach. God's call forms its very identity.

> Many say this is the real battle. Divorce, death, disagreement. But I don't believe it. Oh yes, it's real. And yes, it's a battle. But it's not the main battle. Is the field hospital the main reason for having troops on the field? What's the main reason sergeants are in the trenches? To settle soldiers' disputes? Do chaplains come along just to bury the dead? Or is there a war to be won?
>
> —John Piper, *The Pleasures of God*

Unusual Clarity

When all is said and done, the key for Christ the King Community Church lies in its clarity of purpose and simplicity of operation. We are clear about our mission, vision, values, beliefs, priorities, and expectations. Many traditional churches are in the unfortunate position of having to figure these things out as they go along, and often by committee.

For a Deliberately Simple church, high definition is a by-product of two things: a clear Master and a clear mission. We are not attempting to build our kingdom (small *k*), but his Kingdom (large *K*). God's Kingdom comes when what God wants done gets done.

> Our mandate for world evangelism is the whole Bible. It is to be found in the creation of God (because of which all human beings are responsible to him), in the character of God (as outgoing, loving, compassionate, not willing that any should perish, desiring that all should come to repentance), in the promises of God (that all nations will be blessed through Abraham's seed and will become the Messiah's inheritance), in the Christ of God (now exalted with universal authority, to receive universal acclaim), in the Spirit of God (who convicts of sin, witnesses to Christ, and impels the church to evangelize) and in the church of God (which is a multinational, missionary community, under orders to evangelize until Christ returns).
>
> —John Stott, "The Bible in World Evangelization"

In a Deliberately Simple church, we are rallying around a call from the heart of God. Before Jesus left this earth, he asked us to reach out to as many people as possible before the end of this age. If God didn't have a work for us to do with people, he could have taken us up to heaven immediately.

It's Not about Us

Henry Trumbull, a Sunday school missionary, once said, "Unless a man is ready to work for the salvation of others, it may be questioned whether or not he himself is saved. He who wants only enough religion to save himself is not likely to have even that much." Jesus said, "This is my food, to do the will of my father" (John 4:34). There is really only one thing that God is doing in the world today. God's will is clearly the transformation of the world through the salvation of the lost.

> All authority in heaven and on earth has been given to me. Therefore go and make disciples of all nations, baptizing them in the name of the Father and of the Son and of the Holy Spirit, and teaching them to obey everything I have commanded you. And surely I am with you always, to the very end of the age.
>
> —Matthew 28:18–20

Nothing gets your motor running like giving of yourself for the salvation of others. When you are living to leave a legacy, it stokes the fires of passion.

> To seek pleasure, comfort, and happiness is to guarantee that you will miss them all. On the spiritual as on the natural level, these subjective states become heart-realities only as by-products that come from focusing on something else, something perceived as valuable, invigorating, and commanding. The seeds of happiness, it has been truly said, grow most strongly in the soil of service.
>
> —J. I. Packer, *God's Plans for You*

At CTK our mission statement calls for us "to create an authentic Christian community that effectively reaches out to unchurched people in love, acceptance, and forgiveness so that they may experience the joy of salvation and a purposeful life of discipleship." The most important word in the statement is the word *that*—"that effectively reaches out." We are saying that we are not just going to be an authentic Christian community; we are going to be a certain kind of Christian community, one "that" reaches out.

One New Year's Eve at our Mount Vernon worship center, we held a bash complete with music, dancing, games, and food. It was a fund-raiser for our TREK short-term mission teams. It was a wonderful, fun event (though a not-so-great fund-raiser). The next year, we changed the focus of the event, not so much because we didn't make money for missions but because we looked at it under the lens of our mission statement: "create an authentic Christian community that effectively reaches out to unchurched people ..." We realized that the previous year's event was good for us but didn't have "that." We could see how it could be an effective outreach event if it was repositioned. With a few alterations in the program, we were able to take a good event and make it more purposeful. Our vision now is to see the New Year's Eve Bash become the premier, nonalcoholic party for our community.

Throughout the years, we have found that two kinds of people fit especially well in a Deliberately Simple church: lost people with ruin and wreckage in their lives, and saved people who have a heart to reach out to lost people. If you are looking for a church with programs that will meet your needs, you will likely be disappointed in a Deliberately Simple church. If, on the other hand, you want to find a place where you can contribute to the greatest cause on planet earth, you will have a blast.

> I hear addicts talk about the shakes and panic attacks and the highs and lows of resisting their habit, and to some degree I understand them because I have had habits of my own, but no drug is so powerful as the drug of self. No rut in the mind is so deep as the one that says I am the world, the world belongs to me, all people are characters in my play. There is no addiction so powerful as self-addiction.
>
> —Donald Miller, *Blue Like Jazz*

This is not to say that the Deliberately Simple church is the only church interested in reaching out to a lost world. But there are subtle differences between the traditional and the deliberate forms of outreach. In writing about church planting, Kennon Callahan uses the phrase "preoccupation with us" to describe the traditional church's approach.

> [Here's] what I call the "big bucks" church growth approach to starting new congregations. That approach has four steps: land, minister, members, building.
>
> 1. Land: buy land, hopefully an excellent location for a reasonable price.
> 2. Minister: find a full-time, ordained minister who knows how to start a new church, and with help from the denomination, support his or her salary for the coming five years.
> 3. Members: recruit members to this new congregation.
> 4. Building: build the building, or at least build the first unit of what might be a three- or four-phase building program.
>
> The underlying assumption is that, once we achieve the land, the minister, the members, and the building, then we can figure out more fully what we need to do as our mission. Unfortunately, with this approach the mission sometimes becomes getting the land, finding the minister, recruiting the new members, and building the new building.
>
> On the one hand, I want to confirm that this way of beginning new congregations "works." Land is bought. A competent pastor is found. We recruit new members. We build stage one, stage two, and stage three of our master plan for our buildings. We sponsor many programs and activities for our members. On the other hand, I want to confirm that these four steps seem preoccupied with "us."[7]

That last statement is one of the reasons I am no longer in a traditional church ministry. In the modern-day church, there does seem to be a preoccupation with "us." I got weary of church being about us. It's not about us.

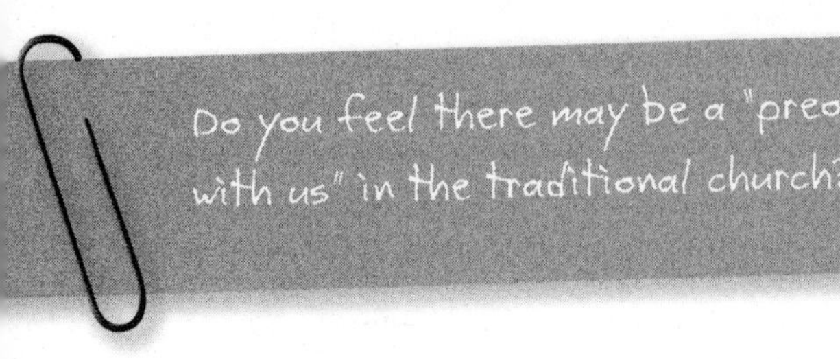

It's about Those Who Are About to Come

There is an important difference between asking people to come to us so we can build a church and asking us to go to them so we can change the world. As Reggie McNeal says, "The shift from 'doing' church at the clubhouse to 'being' church in the world is a paradigm shift that has apparently eluded many church leaders." It's time for God's people to get out of the barn and into the field. It's time for us to quit standing in the barn doorway, inviting the crops to come in.

In a Deliberately Simple church, outreach is intentional. In every church, there are two tensions, outreach (care for those "out there") versus nurture (care for those "in here"). Without deliberate effort, nurture always wins. There are two circles of focus in the church:

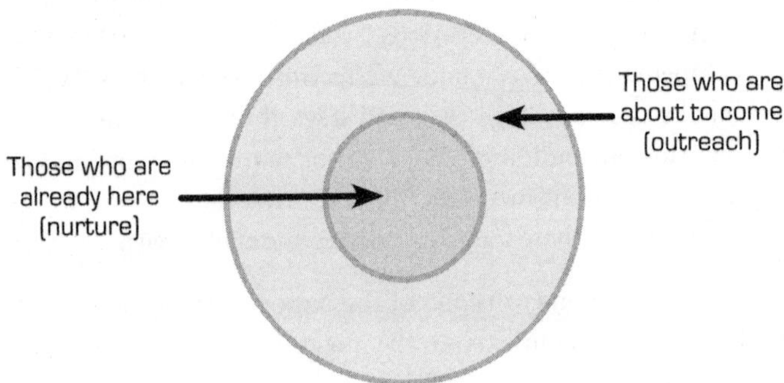

We have a limited amount of time, energy, and resources. Do we put it into us (caring for our needs, our growth and development), or do we put it into others (caring for their needs)? Without intentionality and deliberate effort, we will find ourselves focused on ourselves.

Every church starts out saying, "What if ..." and the rest of the sentence is about how we could reach out. After a while we start saying, "What if ..." and the rest of the sentence is about us. Is it selfishness setting in? I used to think it was a spiritual problem. Now I think it's the natural progression of an organization's life cycle. The longer you are together as a group, the more aware you become of each other's needs, and the more responsive you become to each other's needs. Slowly the arrows get turned in. It is a natural progression. But a natural progression is not what we want. We want a supernatural progression. We want God to help us so lost people are continually prioritized. It's time to love the pitcher less and the water more.

A big part of a pastor's job is to keep the church swimming upstream, because the natural current takes us to a place of inward focus. We buy new chairs not so we will be more comfortable but so our neighbors and friends will be when they finally arrive. We pick songs not with just our ear in mind but for those who are about to come. We don't just want to say that evangelism is a value theoretically. We want it to show up in our priorities.

At the center of any church is the core. The core group takes responsibility to steward the mission, vision, and values and to set direction so the church is faithful to its calling. Surrounding the core is the congregation. The congregation includes those who may not be setting the direction for the church but are in agreement with the direction and are supportive with their time and resources. The third ring is the crowd. The crowd includes everyone who would say that the church is their home regardless of how frequently they attend. This would include weekly attenders as well as people on the margins, such as CEOs (Christmas and Easter Only).

What sets the Deliberately Simple church apart is the outer, fourth ring of constituency: the unchurched. These are people who have not yet attended a worship service or small group meeting, but they will. We may not even know these people yet, but we will get to know them. Maybe this coming week, maybe next month, maybe years from now. But we are preparing for them right now. We include "those who are about to come" in our constituency instead of just those who are already here. If we conceive of our church as only those who are already here, it is easy for an exclusionary membrane to begin to form.

I have had people tell me, "Dave, I don't go to church, but if I ever did, I would check out Christ the King." These are people we will one day see at Christ the King. They have made a mental note, and so have we. We plan with them in mind. With John Wesley, we exclaim, "The world is my parish."

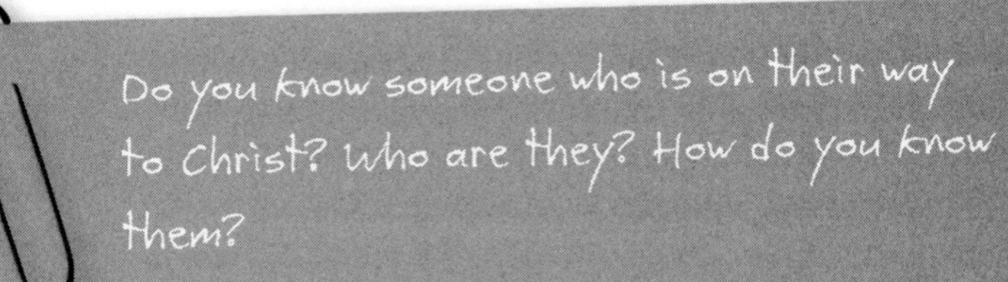

In the early 1990s the people of Christ the King Community Church made a courageous decision. They decided to pave the parking lot. Paving the parking lot might not sound like a big thing to you. But it was a huge decision at the time, the impact of which is still reverberating to this day. At the time, there were about fifty adults in the CTK story. One Sunday morning Pastor Steve Mason looked out the windows and noticed the vehicles in the parking lot, mostly four-wheel drives. The dirt lot was full of potholes and ruts. As Steve describes it, "The parking lot pretty much defined the constituency. If you didn't have four-wheel drive, you weren't going to be able to worship with us." Steve brought the issue up to the people, and the people became concerned. They decided to pave the lot, not for themselves but for those who were about to come. They had already proven that they would come to church with the parking lot in its current condition. They decided to pay the price for others. It cost fifty thousand dollars, a sizeable amount for a group that small. The people gave sacrificially to meet the need. In some cases, people took out second mortgages on their homes. But God honored those sacrifices. The paving of the parking lot was a defining moment of faith, one that continues to bring definition to the CTK story.

Historically, the people of Christ the King have always paid the price for those who are about to come. When we purchased our first set of chairs in Skagit Valley, we said, "We are not making this purchase to make things easier for us. We have already established that we will attend and sit on hard, borrowed chairs. We are buying these chairs for the comfort of those who are about to come." I remind attenders today that before they came, someone paid for the soft chair they are sitting on. We are asking them to "pay it forward" by paying the price for those still on their way.

The apostle Paul wrote, "To the weak I became weak, to win the weak. I have become all things to all men so that by all possible means I might save some" (1 Cor. 9:22). If we were to take on Paul's philosophy, we would say, "I will do what I can to change my ways so I can effectively reach out to others." We can't change the message, but we can change the methods. There are things we can do intentionally to reach the people God has placed around us. We can dress like them. We can talk in plain language. We can respect their time. Our style of music can have the lost person's ear in mind. We can let them know—in our advertising and in our presentation—that there is a place for them here. While some churches say, "Believe and you can belong," we say, "Belong so you can believe." Belonging comes before believing. And we feel that everyone belongs with us, regardless of where they might be on their spiritual journey.

A man from a charismatic background was talking to me about his approach to worship. He said, "I'm going to jump up and down and dance; I don't care what people think." I said to him, "When you were talking about jumping up and down and dancing in the aisles, I was with you. Where you lost me was when you said, 'I don't care what people think.' That doesn't sound like Jesus to me."

When we say we want to be an authentic Christian community that effectively reaches out, we are saying that we do care what people think. We love them enough to forego what may be comfortable for us, to make it comfortable for them.

> If I speak in the tongues of men and of angels, but have not love, I am only a resounding gong or a clanging cymbal.
>
> —1 Corinthians 13:1

We need to balance what works for us with what works for others. We have churches full of people who love Jesus. But that's not enough. We need to love what Jesus loves: the world. If we don't reach out, in effect we are saying to the rest of the world (pardon the frankness), "You can go to hell."

With considerable excitement, a pastor of a traditional church told me about a woman who had started to attend his church. He was particularly excited because the woman was so committed to coming that she had gone shopping to buy new clothes to wear to the church services. I think the pastor was a little taken aback that I didn't share his enthusiasm. To me, it was one of the saddest stories I had heard in a long time. I told him, "I think the wrong people went shopping. You should have told your people to go shopping to come up with a wardrobe that would match hers, not the other way around. We should be paying the price, not them."

Here's a challenging reminder from a portion of Sam Shoemaker's poem "So I Stay Near the Door."

I stay near the door.
I neither go too far in, nor stay too far out.
The door is the most important door in the world—
It is the door through which people walk when they find God.
There's no use my going way inside, and staying there,
When so many are still outside and they, as much as I,
Crave to know where the door is.
And all that so many ever find
Is only the wall where a door ought to be.
They creep along the wall like blind people,
With outstretched, groping hands,
Feeling for a door, knowing there must be a door,
Yet they never find it....
So I stay near the door.

The most tremendous thing in the world
Is for people to find that door—the door to God.
The most important thing anyone can do
Is to take hold of one of those blind, groping hands,
And to put it on the latch—the latch that only clicks
And opens to the person's own touch.
People die outside that door, as starving beggars die
On cold nights in cruel cities in the dead of winter—
Die for want of what is within their grasp.

They live, on the other side of it — live
because they have found it.
Nothing else matters compared to helping
them find it,
And open it, and walk in, and find Him....
So I stay near the door.

From the words we use, to the places we meet, to the clothes we wear, we try to keep the lost in mind. We want to be understandable to them. We are praying for them. We are asking them to come just as they are. We like to say, "We take people where they are; we just don't leave them there." When they arrive, we assume that they are here for a reason, in answer to our prayers.

AN OUTREACH CHURCH

Outreach is developing a lifestyle in which Christ has the freedom to express his nature in us as we develop relationships with friends, neighbors, relatives, and coworkers who don't know him. Outreach is a broad concept, encompassing all the loving expressions we extend, from giving someone a cup of cold water to personally sharing our faith in Jesus. Outreach can include evangelism, but it is far broader. It includes all our outgoing actions of love toward those who have not yet received Christ. Outreach is every attempt on our part to love the lost. Our love is not conditional upon whether they receive Christ or even show interest in doing so. Of course, our heart's desire is for them to become Christians, but unconditional love provides the atmosphere in which they will be most receptive.

Outreach Instead of Evangelism

We like the word *outreach* better than *evangelism*. Evangelism can sometimes be viewed as something that only someone special (like Billy Graham) can do, whereas outreach is something we all can do. Evangelism seems to imply words, while outreach includes deeds. Evangelism has the end in mind, where outreach encompasses the process.

What has been your experience with evangelism?

This distinction between outreach and evangelism is liberating. It frees us from thinking that every contact with a non-Christian must have an overtly evangelistic purpose. It allows us to relax and enjoy the relationship for its own sake. Having this broader perspective, we can focus on people and their needs rather than on their decisions.

Outreach Instead of Seeker

The way we approach reaching out to a lost world is slightly different from that of many other churches that also target the unchurched. We call ourselves an outreach church rather than a seeker church. Let me explain.

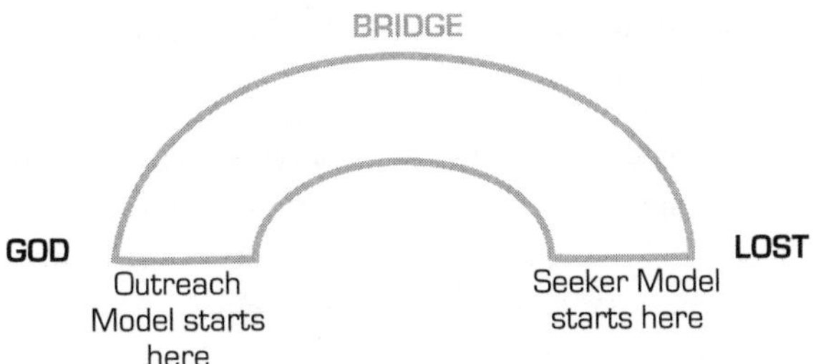

Both the seeker church and the outreach church believe that a bridge needs to be built between God and the lost. They just start building that bridge at different sides of the chasm.

The seeker model begins by thinking about the unchurched person: Who are they? What music do they like? What TV programs do they watch? What don't they like about church? Both Willow Creek Community Church in Illinois and Saddleback Community Church in California, when they began, conducted extensive surveys in their community to find out the answers. Then they structured their ministry accordingly and popularized a model of bridge-building ministry called "seeker-sensitive." The seeker model ends up looking quite different than a traditional church and quite a bit more effective. Many other churches have followed suit, with good results as either a seeker-sensitive or seeker-targeted model.

While we respect the seeker model, a Deliberately Simple church takes a slightly different approach. In the outreach approach, we begin by thinking about God: Who is he? What does he want us to know? How much does he love this world? What price is he willing to pay to reach the lost? Then we clear the path to the cross by removing every obstacle that gets in the way of God's love. When you structure your ministry around outreach, it also ends up looking quite different from a traditional church and quite a bit more effective, at times resembling the seeker church.

Does the starting point matter? Some would say, "As long as you build the bridge, who cares which side you start on?" Truly, the difference is subtle. But it shows up. Two areas where it does are truth telling and worship.

- *Truth telling.* Because we start from a different place, we have less temptation to tinker with or water down the message to make it more palatable for the ears of the nonbeliever. Our mandate is, "What does God want to say?" instead of "What do people want to hear?"
- *Worship.* In seeker services, worship is minimized ("seekers don't know our songs," etc.). In the outreach model, we view true Christian worship as a powerful tool of evangelism

(explored in more detail in the book *Worship Evangelism* by Sally Morganthaler).

Seekers and outreachers should not be confused with the Hatfields and McCoys. There is no animosity between them. Both the seeker and outreach models of ministry fall into a larger class of relevant ministry. Both are driven by a desire to reach as many people as possible as quickly as possible. Both want to honor God by building a bridge to the lost. We just start building in different places.

What could outreachers learn from the seeker movement?

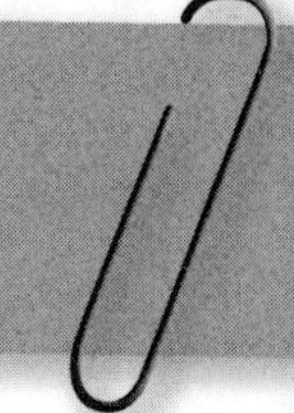

WHOSE JOB IS OUTREACH?

Who is responsible for keeping the arrows pointed out?

Outreach Is the Work of Each Individual

Outreach is not a corporate program as much as it is a personal priority. Outreach is a divine partnership between God and each of his children. We can't do outreach without God. God has chosen not to do it without us.

> What, after all, is Apollos? And what is Paul? Only servants, through whom you came to believe—as the Lord has assigned to each his task.
>
> —1 Corinthians 3:5

The Corinthians came to salvation through the personal ministries of Apollos and Paul. Paul and Apollos, whether they realized it or not, were carrying out assignments. They were the vehicles through which the Corinthians came to believe.

There are divine appointments set up for you, and they're set up for me. It is no mistake that you work where you work, live where you live, and run into the people you run into. We all have a circle of influence. The goal of every believer should be to be a conduit for God's grace for the people God has placed in our lives.

> Be alert to those who are beginning to be awakened by His grace. Seek out those who are on the stretch for God and concentrate energy on their development. I am convinced that a few such persons are within the influence of every Christian.
>
> —William Coleman

> In your hearts set apart Christ as Lord. Always be prepared to give an answer to everyone who asks you to give the reason for the hope that you have. But do this with gentleness and respect.
>
> —1 Peter 3:15

Each believer is called to be an intelligent witness for Christ. The implications of this verse are that (a) we are close enough in relationship that lost people are able to notice a hope in us that they do not possess, and (b) they initiate a conversation with us about that. The posture we keep with prebelievers is critical. We approach them with gentleness and respect.

Outreach Is the Work of Every Small Group

Small groups are a central strategy for our outreach. We ask small groups to remain open instead of becoming closed. Closed groups are groups that, either intentionally or unintentionally, have formed a membrane around themselves that does not allow new people to enter. Sometimes having a closed group is helpful when you are dealing with sensitive issues. Recovery groups are often intentionally closed. But we try to steer our groups away from becoming unintentionally closed. Over time, group members can grow very comfortable with each other, and the tendency is for the group not to recruit new members. Slowly the group's motto can become, "Us four, no more."

Open groups, on the other hand, are eager and ready to accept new people. They balance the impulse for community with the mandate to reach out. To help maintain this balance, we ask each small group to pray over "the empty chair" as a symbolic reminder that there are people around us who need what we have. This prayer, usually at the end of a group meeting, is that God will lead us to someone new whom we can love, someone we can invite to be a part of our group. We have found that this is a prayer God loves to answer, "for the Son of Man came to seek and to save what was lost" (Luke 19:10).

The story of the *Titanic* expresses the lifesaving potential of every small group. On the night of April 15, 1912, the *Titanic* disappeared beneath the surface of the North Atlantic. The unsinkable ship had betrayed those who trusted her. With only twenty lifeboats available, hundreds of people were left to perish.

The lifeboats, some only partially filled, rowed to safety beyond the desperate reach of those struggling in the icy waters. The justification for not helping the drowning was that the lifeboats might be capsized.

Lifeboat 14 chose a different course. Following the cries in the darkness, they returned to save a precious few. Their reward was knowing they had risked all to save some. Others would live with regret because they failed to reach out. But not the crew of Lifeboat 14. When called upon in the moment of need, they did the right thing for the right reason.

We ask every small group to be a lifeboat instead of a pleasure boat. We don't want to become so comfortable with our own salvation that we no longer hear the cries of the people drowning all around us. At Christ the King we are "theological schizophrenics" when it comes to outreach. On one hand, we know that God is at work through every church and ministry to build his kingdom. On the other hand, we are acting as if there were no one else around and if we don't do it, no one will.

Outreach Is the Work of Every Worship Center

At Christ the King we have identified three priorities: worship, small groups, and outreach. Typically, in a worship center there is a director of both worship and small groups. Who is the outreach director? The pastor. The pastor sees to it that outreach happens through everything we do, including worship and small groups.

The Deliberately Simple church is not interested in building a large, centralized compound to which everyone is invited to come. We are looking to decentralize the church—to push it out instead of pull 'em in.

> You will receive power when the Holy Spirit comes on you; and you will be my witnesses in Jerusalem, and in all Judea and Samaria, and to the ends of the earth.
>
> —Acts 1:8

In the first-century church, the arrows were clearly pointed out. Starting with the local community (Jerusalem) and moving to the surrounding region (Judea), extending to the neighboring region (Samaria), and ultimately to the ends of the earth, the church was on the go.

The question, it seems to me, is this: is church a place you go to, or is church a place you go from? When you are a part of an outreach church, church is a place you go from.

PASSION FOR PEOPLE

Churches typically engage in very similar activities. What differentiates churches from each other is their values: both the content of those values and the strength of conviction with which they are held. A Deliberately Simple church is characterized by a passion for people instead of institutional inertia.

When Cortez landed in Mexico, he set fire to the ships that brought him there. It was either conquer or be conquered. There was no turning back. His heart was completely in it. His fervor reflected his faith; his passion corresponded with his profession.

If you had only one word to define passion, it would be *heart*. The dictionary defines passion as "intense emotion compelling action. A strong devotion to some object, activity or concept." It is a fire in the belly.

> We do not lose heart. Though outwardly we are wasting away, yet inwardly we are being renewed day by day.
>
> —2 Corinthians 4:16

> Whatever you do, work at it with all your heart, as working for the Lord, not for men.
>
> —Colossians 3:23

You can go a long way with the right heart. The Pike's Place Fish Market in Seattle has become the most well-known fish market in the world by bringing a contagious enthusiasm and energy to their site. Their workers dance, sing, toss fish, and otherwise carry on. They are thoroughly immersed in their work. They have proven that it's not just what you do; it's how you do it.

In *Zen and the Art of Motorcycle Maintenance*, Robert Pirsig refers to this vigor as "gumption."

> If you're going to repair a motorcycle, an adequate supply of gumption is the first and most important tool. If you haven't got that, you might as well gather up all the other tools and put them away, because they won't do you any good. Gumption is the psychic gasoline that keeps the whole thing going. If you haven't got it, there's no way the motorcycle can possibly be fixed. But if you have got it and know how to keep it, there's absolutely no way in the

> whole world that motorcycle can keep from getting fixed. It's bound to happen. Therefore the thing that must be monitored at all times and preserved before anything else is gumption.

At a writer's workshop, the moderator asked a panel of well-known authors this question: "What does it take to write a best-seller?" After little discussion, their consensus was that writers must be *in a fury*. If you write with passion, your words are intensified. Your message has force. Your readers can better sense your spirit and sincerity. The authors went on to suggest that if you cannot write with passion, perhaps you have selected the wrong subject.

Followers of Jesus Christ have certainly selected the right subject. And if passion, gumption, or fury (or whatever you want to call it) is important to selling fish, maintaining motorcycles, or writing novels, it is certainly appropriate for something as important as God's work.

> This is the true joy in life ... being used for a purpose recognized as a mighty one. I am of the opinion that my life belongs to the whole community and as long as I live it is my privilege to do for it whatever I can. I want to be thoroughly used up when I die.... Life is no brief candle to me. It's a sort of splendid torch which I've got to hold up for the moment and I want to make it burn as brightly as possible before handing it on to future generations.
>
> —George Bernard Shaw, *Man and Superman*

Real passion is not optional for a Deliberately Simple church. If this were poker, we would be all in. We believe that what is going on in the church is the most important thing happening in the world. For this reason, we are highly motivated and tenacious.

Enthusiasm for what we're doing is nearly as critical as what we're doing. Søren Kierkegaard warned of the danger of the church losing its passion for the gospel and treating it like just another piece of information. The result for the church could be compared to reading a cookbook to a hungry person.

When unchurched people come to church, one of their leading questions is, "Do they really believe this stuff?" Visitors are looking to see whether we are lip-synching or whether it's coming from the heart. Unfortunately, the unbelieving world has concluded that Christians are going through the motions.

Several years ago at Christmas, my wife, Kristyn, and I flew to my home state of Alaska—and we got out of there just in time. A volcano erupted south of Anchorage and threatened to disrupt air travel. As it turned out, we were fortunate to make our flight back to Seattle, but those scheduled to fly during the next couple of days were grounded by the fallout.

In the aftermath, my parents mailed me a clipping from a newspaper in Anchorage. A photographer had gone into the air terminal and taken a picture of one of the monitors that displays the airline departure times. The picture had no caption. It spoke for itself, because the monitor read,

Flight	**Status**
1727	Cancelled
362	Cancelled
1742	Cancelled
584	Cancelled
1720	Cancelled
1557	Cancelled

1714	Cancelled
1717	Cancelled
1724	Cancelled
Delta Airlines, We Love to Fly, and It Shows!	

Sometimes there is a disconnect between what we advertise and what we're really all about. I remember coming up behind a car on the interstate. On the back of the car was a bumper sticker: "Happiness is being a grandmother." So with enthusiasm I began to pass, expecting to see the sweetest grandmotherly figure behind the wheel of that car. What I saw instead was an older lady hunched over the steering wheel, with a bulldog-like scowl on her face. I couldn't tell if it was the grandma or the big, bad wolf in the grandmother's clothes. And I thought, "That's false advertising … to say that happiness is being a grandmother and then to look like that!"

I realize that as Christians we can be guilty of false advertising from time to time. We say we love to fly, but what shows is that we are spiritually grounded. Nothing is taking off. All flights are cancelled. We profess that happiness is being a Christian, but most people could never guess that we're enjoying ourselves. We resemble Eeyore more than Tigger. All the slogans and bumper stickers can't disguise the reality that there is a disconnect between our profession and our passion.

> Compared with what we ought to be we are only half awake. Our fires are damped; our drafts are checked.
>
> —William James

How do you keep the fire lit in your life?

When we lack passion, it is often because we have allowed something precious to become familiar. If Satan can desensitize us, he can effectively undermine what God wants to do in our lives. We keep the fires of passion lit by keeping clear about what is important: the salvation of the lost.

THE ELEVENTH COMMANDMENT

After a woman visited Christ the King Community Church for the first time, she told the friend who invited her, "This can't be church. Everyone is so real." When I heard that, I had mixed emotions: happy, because the word *authentic* is in our mission statement; sad, because when outsiders think of the church, they evidently think "artificial" or "hypocritical" or "contrived." It is because of the perceived disconnect between church and "real" that we have added a commandment, commandment number eleven: Keep it real.

Say Goodbye to Impression Management

The church I grew up in was unreal in many ways. We would wear clothes to church that we never wore any other time (except maybe to funerals). We would hear a style of music on Sunday that we would not listen to the rest of the week. At church we would speak in ways that we did not speak the rest of the week. It was the only time that we would sit on hard wooden benches (other than in the Little League dugout, and we didn't much like sitting on the bench there either). Around the "church people" we would act differently—more upright, more spiritual. We would act nicer than we really were. It was classic impression management. After church I remember retreating to the car, closing the door behind me, and breathing a huge sigh of relief. The duplicity was killing me.

When I was a kid, the solution that was proposed to rectify the discrepancy between how we lived our life on Sunday at church and how we lived the rest of the week was to act just as strangely Monday through Saturday as we did on Sunday. The solution I've come to as an adult is just the opposite: be the same person on Sunday that you are Monday through Saturday. It seems to be working out a lot better.

Stephen Covey, in his book *The Seven Habits of Highly Effective People*, chronicles the tectonic shift in American culture from a "character ethic" to a "personality ethic." This is the shift that has taken place in the culture in the past one hundred years. Businesses have shifted resources from research and development to marketing and public relations. Politicians have become more concerned with sound bites and slogans than with policies and platforms. This is the age of style over substance. The church is not immune.

Some of what I see in evangelicalism reminds me of a conversation I had with a friend after she auditioned for a reality TV show. I asked her how it went. She said, "Not so good." I asked her why. She said, "They wanted me to be meaner. They tried to coach me to be nastier to the other people in the cast. But I just couldn't do it. I am who I am." Remember, this is supposed to be a *reality* TV show. Even the reality is staged.

In a Deliberately Simple church, we want our energy to go into experiencing and expressing the grace of God, not into impression management. Ray Stedman's book *Authentic Christianity* has a section called "The Big Lie" that is especially probing.

> The flesh, or natural life, likes nothing better than to hide or disguise itself. We all tend to fear rejection if we are

> seen for what we are. The Satanic lie is that in order to be liked or accepted we must appear capable or successful. Therefore we either project capability (the extrovert) or we seek to hide our failure (the introvert). The new covenant offers the opposite. If we will admit our inadequacy, we can have God's adequacy, and all we have sought vainly to produce (confidence, success, impact, integrity, and reality) is given to us at the point of our inability. The key is to take away the veil.

Christians, saved by grace, should be the first ones to take away the veil. After all, God loves us as we are. We can live in reality, knowing that we have nothing to lose and nothing to prove.

Say Hello to Candor

Most people appreciate genuineness and candor. Churches characterized by Deliberate Simplicity prefer authenticity, with its warts and wrinkles, to religious veneer. God can work with honesty. What he appears to despise is phoniness. After all, Jesus saved his most stinging rebukes for hypocrites.

When you've got candor—and you'll never *completely* get it—everything just operates faster and better. Candor works because candor unclutters. It's what the Bible calls having our yes be yes and our no be no.

> What happened at a suburban cocktail party we attended recently is classic. Over white wine and sushi rolls, one woman standing in a cluster of five others started lamenting the horrible stress being endured by the local elementary school's music teacher. Other guests chimed in, all agreeing that fourth-graders were enough to send you to the insane asylum. Fortunately, just before the music teacher was canonized, another guest entered the conversation, saying, "Are you guys crazy? That teacher gets fifteen weeks off a year!" She pointed to the doctor standing

> in the circle, who had been nodding away in agreement. "Robert," she said, "you make life-and-death decisions every day. Surely you don't buy this sad story, do you?" Talk about killing polite chitchat. The new guest sent everyone scattering, mostly toward the bar.
>
> —Jack Welch, *Winning*

Candor can unnerve people. But it shouldn't unnerve us as much as it does. Why do we have to use so many euphemisms in church? Why can't we say *addict* instead of *struggling*? Why can't we use the word *adultery* instead of *unfaithful*? We say we want to protect others, but maybe we just want to protect ourselves—from having to get real about ourselves and the world around us.

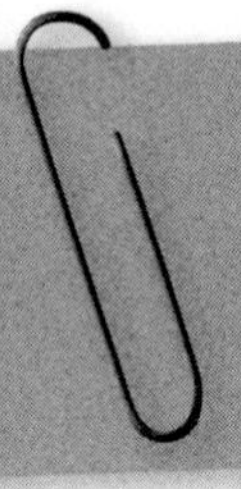

In the average evangelical church, do you think it would be emotionally safe to reveal that you have failed morally?

WYSIWYG

The reality we are after—to borrow from the world of computers—is WYSIWYG (what you see is what you get). We want our personal and public presentation to be sincere. The word *sincere* is a compound from Latin (*sina* + *cera*) that literally means "without wax." The phrase comes out of a culture where pottery was a cornerstone of commerce. When hairline cracks would begin to emerge on a piece of pottery, some sellers would fill those cracks with wax to fake out the buyer by giving the piece a smooth, polished finish. Discerning shoppers would often take a piece of pottery out into the sunlight, where they could see if light would shine through the wax. To save shoppers the trouble, merchants began to hang a small sign: "*Sina Cera.*" The shopper would be assured that a *sina cera* piece of pottery would be minus the touch-up.

What impressions do you think unchurched people would form about authenticity by watching Christian television?

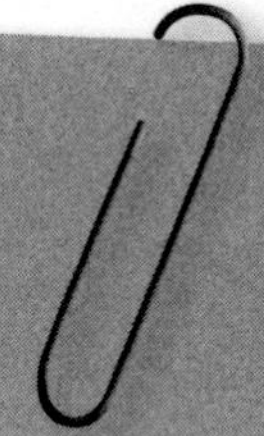

Comedian George Burns offered up this cynical take on our world: "Sincerity is the key. When you can fake that, you've got it made." Deliberate Simplicity advocates that we can make progress by simply being who we really are. Real sincerity stands in sharp contrast to a Christian subculture whose motto appears to be, "Fake it 'til you make it" or "The show must go on." Sadly, the twenty-first-century church may be at the same place pro wrestling used to be when people wondered if it was real or staged. But then the World Wrestling Federation said, "We want to fake it *in an authentic way*" and has ended up being more real than some churches and Christian organizations I've seen.

Subtract the Unnecessary

The problem with today's church is not that it doesn't have the right stuff. It's all the other stuff it's got. The experience in modern churches is not unlike going to lunch with a friend and watching her order coffee. After putting in a couple sugar packets, a couple creamers, and an ice cube, she ends up with an off-white concoction that looks and tastes a bit different than coffee. You feel like asking, "Would you like some coffee to go with your 'coffee'?" Likewise, the modern church has so many artificial additives that you feel like asking, "Would you like some Christianity to go with your 'Christianity'?"

> Addition is the exercise of fools. Subtraction is the exercise of genius.
>
> —Tom Peters

> Perfection is not achieved when there is nothing more to add, but when there is nothing left to take away.
>
> —Antoine de Saint Exupery

Deliberate Simplicity is about removing unnecessary pretense to get down to what is real. It's about continually paring down the extraneous to get back to the essential.

THE GENUINE ARTICLE

The first-century church was the genuine article. We read in Acts 2:45 that "they gave to anyone as he had need." They were not so heavenly minded that they were of no earthly good. We read, "They broke bread in their homes and ate together with glad and sincere hearts" (v. 46). They were not getting together in a pious, artificial environment called church. Church was happening in their lives ... at the dinner table ... in their homes. There is a steep unlearning curve for a church courageous enough to keep it real. This is why we talk in terms of *deliberate* simplicity.

"Real" Means "Imperfect"

In the average evangelical church in America today, you will hear jargon like "relationships," "community," and "authenticity." Upon closer inspection, you will find that as with fur, the variety being worn is faux: made in imitation of a natural material.

A men's ministry leader I have encountered speaks often about authenticity. I've never been around him except that he has spoken with me about being authentic. Oddly, I don't think I really know this guy. The more he talks about being authentic, the less he seems authentic to me. Something is not natural here. Certainly, inauthenticity is a judgment call, but as Robert Moog, inventor of the synthesizer, said, "You can make vinyl look like walnut, but when you get up close to it, you can tell it's not real."

The text of an advertisement we created at CTK reinforces our value of authenticity: "Do you know what's special about us? Nothing. Absolutely nothing. If you are looking for a perfect church, where people talk, act, and dress perfectly, you are going to be severely disappointed with us. At CTK you'll find real people, with real problems, real blue jeans, and a real God who we're learning to love. What you won't find is: extra reverb so that we sound 'holier than thou,' music written during someone else's lifetime, harsh judgmentalism implying we don't struggle but you do. We found out that we're all made out of the same stuff. There's nothing special about us. So bring your story, your pain, your questions, your sense of humor. You'll fit right in."

A friend of mine attends an evangelical church with a large emphasis on community. It seems forced to me. The "relationships" they emphasize are too rehearsed, too cheesy, too perfect. The people seem plastic to me. They dress the same, talk the same, and act the same. It appears manufactured and contrived. We want human and honest. Listen to Gordon MacKenzie, in his book *Orbitting the Giant Hairball*, describe the lack of authenticity that he experienced when a woman tried out for a job as a news reporter.

> Taking her cues from our video, playing on a TV monitor, the woman began to read her narration. It was awful. Well, actually, it was perfect. That's why it was awful. We didn't want perfect. I had tried to tell her that. Perfect is not real. Perfect is not interesting. We wanted real. Conversational. Imperfect. Authentic. It was very hard to get this across to what turned out to be our professional announcers.
>
> No, that's not right. They understood right away. What was hard for them was to let go of their announcer

training and be real. They both eventually rediscovered their authentic voices, but not before we heard take after take of flawless readings that were all, alas, devoid of the taste of humanness.

What some churches have created is a remarkably sophisticated, very efficient system dedicated to creating the surface appearance of people-centricity, while in reality remaining as unresponsive, impenetrable, and clueless regarding the real needs of its people as even the most backward car dealer. The emerging culture is looking for something far less slick and produced. People are not looking for someone to speak to them glibly about relationships. They are looking for a friend. They are not looking for someone to talk with them about getting real. They are looking for those who will be open and honest about their lives.

To keep from faux relationships, I believe that important corollaries to "community" and "authenticity" are "natural" and "imperfect." If it's the real thing, it will often have a most natural feel to it. If it's the real thing, it will probably be imperfect. A wallet I once purchased held a little slip of paper inside that read,

> Your wallet is made of real leather. Unlike artificial or simulated leather, authentic leather may have imperfections and variety in coloration or texture. These are not indications of defect. These are marks of distinction. You are the owner of a genuine leather article.

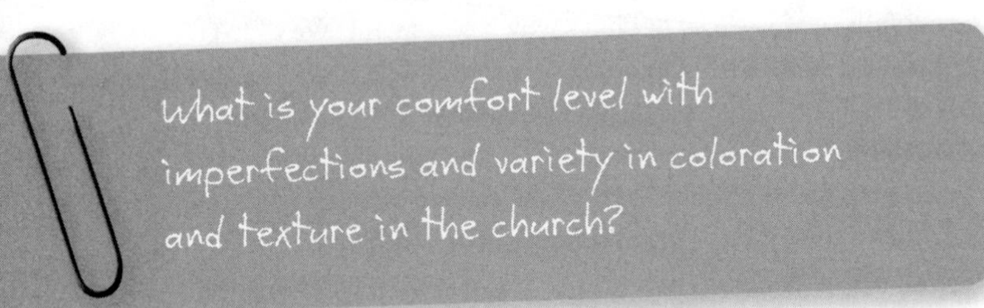

You Can Smell It

The difference in atmosphere in an authentic Christian community is palpable. You walk in and you can smell that something's different. In one of Paul's writings, he speaks to Christians about this distinction.

> Thanks be to God, who always leads us in triumphal procession in Christ and through us spreads everywhere the fragrance of the knowledge of him. For we are to God the aroma of Christ among those who are being saved and those who are perishing. To the one we are the smell of death; to the other, the fragrance of life. And who is equal to such a task? Unlike so many, we do not peddle the word of God for profit. On the contrary, in Christ we speak before God with sincerity, like men sent from God.
>
> —2 Corinthians 2:14–17

How do we know that Paul is sincere? The words Paul uses appeal to your olfactory senses—fragrance, aroma. That is, you can smell it. Aroma and fragrance are metaphors for feelings that transcend physical description, for the almost indescribable feeling that can accompany certain places and people. When it's real, you can sense it. When it's too polished, you start to smell something else.

> Some books on salesmanship recommend that persuaders try to mirror the posture or talking styles of their clients in order to establish rapport. But that's been shown not to work. It makes people more uncomfortable, not less. It's too obviously phony.
>
> —Malcolm Gladwell, *Blink*

Could church conferences fixated on methodology unwittingly push the church away from authenticity?

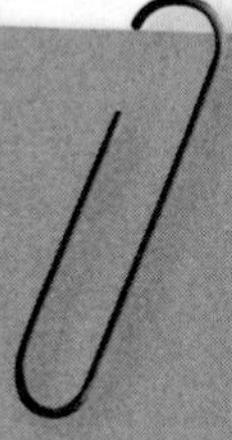

IT'S NOT A RELIGION; IT'S A RELATIONSHIP

The original church was simply a community of people devoted to knowing and loving God and knowing and loving one another. They were meeting regularly in homes and public places to worship, teach, and pray. "They devoted themselves to the apostles' teaching and to the fellowship, to the breaking of bread and to prayer" (Acts 2:42).

Activity for God can be the greatest enemy of devotion to him. This is one of the reasons we try to prune the activity branches at CTK, so God has our time and attention. We don't want our worship of God to be just a foil for our self-absorption. Following Christ is not about religion; it's about relationship. When Jesus was quizzed about the most important commandment, he replied, "'Love the Lord your God with all your heart and with all your soul and with all your mind.' This is the first and greatest commandment. And the second is like it: 'Love your neighbor as yourself.' All the Law and the Prophets hang on these two commandments" (Matt. 22:37–40).

Jesus said that everything that really matters can be summarized in two concise but potent statements: "Love the Lord your God with all your heart" and "Love your neighbor as yourself." He said you can take all the commands in Scripture (over seven hundred in the Old Testament and four hundred in the New Testament) and hang them on these two pegs: love God and love people. If we love God and people well, the commandments take care of themselves. If we feel the right way about God and people, we will do the right things for God and people. If we truly love God, we are not going to have other gods before him or take his name in vain. If we truly love people, we are not going to lie, steal, commit adultery, or covet. If our hearts are in the right place, our actions will naturally follow.

It's about Loving God

The first commandment is, "You shall have no other gods before me" (Exod. 20:3). Deuteronomy 10:12 expands the thought: "And now, O Israel, what does the LORD your God ask of you but to fear the LORD your God, to walk in all his ways, to love him, to serve the LORD your God with all your heart and with all your soul." Jesus challenged us in Mark 12:30 to "Love the Lord your God with all your heart and with all your soul and with all your mind and with all your strength." One of the primary ways we keep it real simple is by keeping our focus on God, not on our processes, programs, or productions. We want to be believers with blinders.

The name of our church, Christ the King Community Church, reminds us whose church this really is. Christ the King is an inherently propositional and edifying phrase. It reminds us where our loyalties ultimately lie. I remember having a conversation with some men about the name Christ the King Community Church. They didn't see the name as very user-friendly. I had to agree. It is a mouthful. It doesn't fit really well on a business card. But I said in reply with tongue firmly in cheek, "Our church was named for our founder. If our founder were dead, I would feel more comfortable about changing the name. But our founder is alive."

The key word and the formidable challenge of the greatest commandment is *all*. All your heart. All your soul. All your mind. All your strength. Spiritual integrity is a tall order! Integrity is "an unimpaired or unmarred condition, soundness, utter sincerity, candor, avoidance of deception, lack of artificiality, being complete and undivided." It is related to the word *integer*—a whole number (no fractions or percentages). In baking, we say that bread has integrity when all the parts touch, when a loaf is of equal consistency. Integrity is the difference between bread and the ingredients that make up bread. Integrity means we have not compartmentalized our lives. To the extent that there is inconsistency, we lack integrity. So when we say it's all about God but then act like it's all about us, we are not loving God the way we should.

In the mid-1800s C. T. Studd was a wealthy aristocrat and one of the greatest cricket players in England. He also became a model of lordship in his day and age. F. B. Meyer was a Baptist preacher and pastor of Christ Church in the heart of London at that time. Studd and Meyer had a discussion about spiritual power, which seemed to attend Studd's ministry, but not that of Pastor Meyer. The conversation was recounted in Meyer's sermon, "Where Is It?"

> I said to Charles Studd: "What is the difference between you and me? You seem so happy, and I somehow am in the trough of the wave." He replied: "There is nothing that I have got which you may not have, Mr. Meyer." But I asked: "How am I to get it?" "Well," he said, "have you given yourself right up to God?"
>
> I winced. I knew that if it came to that, there was a point where I had been fighting my deepest convictions for months. I had lived away from it, but when I came to the Lord's table and handed out the bread and wine, then it met me; or when I came to a convention or meeting of holy people, something stopped me as I remembered this. It was the one point where my will was entrenched. I thought I would do something with Christ that night which would settle it one way or the other, and I met Christ.
>
> You will forgive a man who owes everything to one night in his life if to help other men he opens his heart for a moment. I knelt in my room and gave Christ the ring of my will with the keys on it, but kept one little key back, the key of a closet in my heart, in one back story in my heart. He said to me, "Are they all here?" And I said: "All but one." "What is that?" said He. "It is the key of a little cupboard," said I, "in which I have got something which Thou needest not interfere with, but it is mine."
>
> Then, as He put the keys back into my hand, and seemed to be gliding away to the door, He said: "My child, if you cannot trust Me with all, you do not trust Me at all." I cried: " Stop," and He seemed to come back; and holding the little key in my hand, in thought I said: "I cannot give it, but if Thou wilt take it Thou shalt have it."

> He took it, and within a month from that time He had cleared out that little cupboard of things which had been there for months. I knew He would.... Imagine myself being such a fool as nearly to have sold my birthright for that mess of pottage.[8]

The most miserable people I know are Christians wrestling with God over a key. Once all the keys are handed over, your life can begin. Chuck Colson said it so well when he said, "The greatest challenge facing the church today is to reassert the Lordship of Christ." Lordship is making God number one in your life. It is the first and greatest commandment: God first.

How do you react to the statement, "If Christ is not Lord of all, he is not Lord at all"?

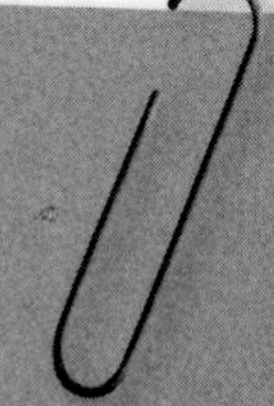

It's about Loving People

While Christianity is fundamentally about a love relationship with God, if all we do is love Jesus, we will fall short. Christ calls us to an others-centered spirituality. When Jesus was asked to name the most important commandment, he said in effect, "Let me give you the top two instead: Love God with all your heart, and love your neighbor as yourself." Jesus knew that if he said, "It's all about loving God," then we would think, "It's about us and God," which would really mean, "It's all about us." So Jesus said, "Closely following on the heels of our love for God should be a love for others." Healthy spirituality balances passion for God with a compassion for people that prays, "Lord, help me live from day to day in such a self-forgetful way that even when I kneel to pray my prayer will be for others."

Deliberate Simplicity keeps us in touch with the truth that this is really all about people. People come before programs, policies, or protocol. It's not about buildings. It's not about budgets. It's not about organizational structures. It's about real people having a real relationship with God, and real relationships with each other.

COME AS YOU ARE . . . REALLY

The one charge that has never been leveled against the Bible is that its characters are not real people. Even its greatest heroes, like David, are presented so unvarnished, so "warts and all," that the book of Samuel has been called the most honest historical writing of the ancient world.

In churches characterized by Deliberate Simplicity, you often hear that what is most attractive about them is the openness and honesty of the people. There are no pretensions, no attempts by people to be something they are not. Consequently, it is possible to relax, to be vulnerable, to admit your own hurts and problems, knowing you will be accepted rather than judged.

In Luke 15 we read the story of the prodigal son. It is a story of failure and redemption. It is a story of waywardness and grace. When the son returns, his father throws him a party to celebrate. The father gives him a robe, a ring, and new sandals. The older brother isn't really happy about all this. After all, he has been faithfully carrying out his duties while the other son has been wandering. Max Lucado, in his book *Come Thirsty*, fills us in on the "rest of the story." This is fictitious, but it rings true.

> Do you know what happened next?... The older brother resolves to rain on the forgiveness parade.
>
> "Nice robe there, little brother," he tells him one day. "Better keep it clean. One spot and Dad will send you to the cleaners with it."

The younger brother waves him away, but the next time he sees the father, he quickly checks his robe for stains.

A few days later big brother warns about the ring. "Quite a piece of jewelry Dad gave you. He prefers that you wear it on the thumb."

"The thumb. He didn't tell me that."

"Some things we're just supposed to know."

"But it won't fit my thumb."

"What's your goal—pleasing our father or your own personal comfort?" the spirituality monitor gibes, walking away.

Big brother isn't finished. With the pleasantness of a dyspeptic IRS auditor, he taunts, "If Dad sees you with loose laces, he'll take the sandals back."

"He will not. They were a gift. He wouldn't ... would he?" The ex-prodigal then leans over to snug the strings. As he does, he spots a smudge on his robe. Trying to rub it off, he realizes the ring is on a finger, not his thumb. That's when he hears his father's voice, "Hello, Son."

From the father's perspective, it's about the relationship, pure and simple. God does not love us because of who we are or what we do. God loves us in spite of who we are and what we do. There is nothing we can do to make God love us more. There is nothing we can do to make God love us less. The fact that God loves us isn't really much of a commentary on who we are at all. It is a commentary on who God is. He simply does not give us what we deserve. He gives us grace. According to A. W. Tozer, "Grace is the good pleasure of God, which causes him to bestow benefit upon the undeserving."

I remember an older-brother-type Christian saying to me, "Man, you guys at Christ the King will take anybody!" He did not mean that as a compliment, but I've worn that comment as a badge of honor. It's true. We pray that God will send us the last, least, lost, and lonely, the broken, burned, bypassed, and bored.

We don't care where you've been or what you've done; we have a culture of recovery. The church is a hospital, not a showcase. At Christ the King we like to say, "God will take you where you are. He just won't leave you where you are."

Sinners occasionally come to church, either to a small group or a worship center. We love it when they do. We are praying that God will send us people with ruin and wreckage in their lives. But this is where spiritual schizophrenia can set in if we're not careful, because people with ruin and wreckage come with, well, ruin and wreckage. They have lifestyle issues that can range from the inappropriate to the illicit to the illegal. Reaching out to sinners can be a messy proposition, to be sure. Sin really does a number on people, and the impact is often profound. So how do we respond to those broken by sin? We roll out the red carpet. We get on the intercom and say four very important words: "Come as you are."

That four-word phrase is critical to what God is doing in the CTK story. We say those words through our byline, "Always a place for you." We say those words through our motto, "Forgiveness for the past, hope for the future." We say those words through our mission statement, "An authentic Christian community that effectively reaches out to unchurched people in love, acceptance, and forgiveness." I suspect that God has been gracious to us partly because we have said to those broken by their sin, "Come as you are." Deep down I believe that God will withdraw his hand of favor if we ever roll up the red carpet or are no longer willing to say those words.

Our pastors are occasionally asked what our posture is toward certain groups of sinners — whether they are allowed in our small groups or worship centers. One answer fits all: "Come as you are." God can change lives. God can work miracles. We are just trying to set up an environment where people can be exposed to the powerful, life-changing grace of God. At CTK you can belong before you believe.

At CTK we do not have categories of sinners. There are only people. People like me. People like you. People like us. People who desperately need God's grace. Everyone is welcome to receive that grace. God will take you where you are. He just won't leave you where you are. To invite people into that life-altering journey, we say, "Come as you are."

Is the church supposed to be a showcase or a hospital? We know what it is supposed to be. But what is it in reality? The answer might become clearer when you take a category of sin (think of a good one) and ask whether or not a person with that condition can get in the doors of your worship center. If it's a hospital, they'll be more than welcome. If it's a showcase, you might be thinking twice. Jesus made it clear that he came for sinners, for folks with hurts, habits, and hang-ups. How clear are we?

What fuels the environment of grace at CTK? Redeemed leaders. Many of the leaders of our minimovement have fallen hard along the way. There are former swindlers, murderers, and adulterers among our key leaders. Speaking for myself, I am very undeserving to be God's child, much less a leader in his kingdom. But that is what grace is—undeserved favor. I know that if God can take me out of the miry clay and set my feet upon a rock, he can do that for anyone.

Many of us live in fear that we have to be well manicured to keep the robe, the ring, and the sandals. Christ died for you. Not for who you will become. Who you are. When it comes to our salvation, we have nothing to lose and nothing to prove. You can be who you are. It's not about what you do. It's about what God has already done. He has given us a new identity as his children. We are fellow strugglers, but we are bound for glory.

Where does our dysfunctional commitment to posing and artificiality come from? It is facilitated, in part, by the many teachers who work so hard to instill a professionalism that prizes correctness over authenticity. Brennan Manning, in his *Ragamuffin Gospel*, offers this diagnosis:

> Each of us pays a heavy price for our fear of falling flat on our faces. It assures the progressive narrowing of

our personalities and prevents exploration and experimentation. As we get older we do only the things we do well. There is no growth in Christ Jesus without some difficulty and fumbling. If we are going to keep on growing, we must keep on risking failure throughout our lives. When Max Planck was awarded the Nobel Prize for his discovery of quantum theory, he said, "Looking back over the long and labyrinthine path which finally led to the discovery, I am vividly reminded of Goethe's saying that men will always be making mistakes as long as they are striving for something."

You know, in spite of the fact that Christianity speaks of the cross, redemption and sin, we're unwilling to admit failure in our own lives. Why? Partly because it's human nature's defense mechanism against its own inadequacies. But even more so, it's because of the successful image our culture demands of us. There are some real problems with projecting the perfect image. First of all, it's simply not true—we are not always happy, optimistic, in command. Second, projecting the flawless image keeps us from reaching people who feel we just wouldn't understand them. And third, even if we could live a life with no conflict, suffering, or mistakes, it would be a shallow existence.[9]

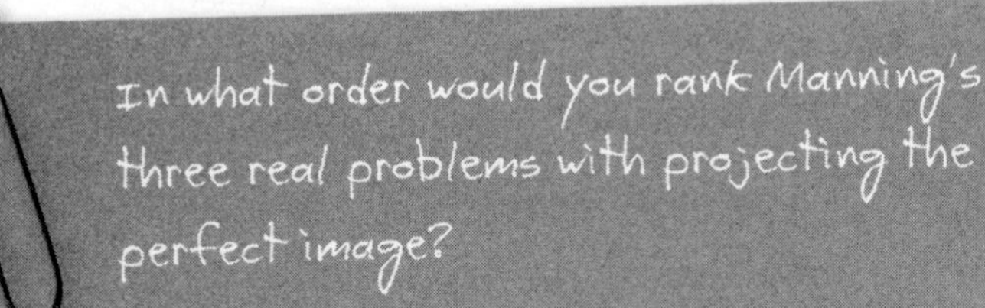

We pay a high price for our lack of comfort with imperfection, either in others or in ourselves. A Deliberately Simple church takes a realistic approach to spiritual formation. We understand that discipleship is a process. We accept that we are not perfect, yet. On one hand, we want to be like Jesus. On the other hand, we're not Jesus. A Latin phrase that fed Martin Luther's theology was *simul justus et peccator* ("simultaneously saint and sinner"). So be who you really are. God can take you from there.

INFORMALITY

The eleventh commandment (Keep it real) applies not only to substance but also to style. Members of the early church "broke bread in their homes and ate together with glad and sincere hearts" (Acts 2:46). Often, being real means taking a less-formal approach.

One of our first approaches to assimilating people into small groups at CTK was a demonstration of Deliberate Simplicity. CTK first met in a rented Elks Lodge in Mount Vernon, Washington. On an auditorium wall was an elk's head. In the early months, after each service I would ask those who were new to meet me under the elk's head. Folks would gather with me, and we would make some brief introductions. I would then ask if anyone would be available to facilitate a new small group, and if someone would be willing to open their home for the group to meet. Invariably, I would get a positive response. Then I would ask if we could meet that week, say on Wednesday. I'd ask everyone to exchange phone numbers on the spot, and I'd tell them I'd see them at the host's home that week. To this day, we have never developed a better assimilation strategy than those cheesy, impromptu "under the elk's head" meetings.

> Before we went public, I used to send out a company-wide joke each day, just as a way of loosening things up. The day after the IPO, I sat down at my computer to write that day's joke and in walked the general counsel. He says to me, "You know that joke of the day thing? I think it's very funny." Gosh, thank you, I replied. "Well, stop it," he said.

> We're a public company now, and we don't want to offend anyone. If you want to keep sending out jokes, they can only be about lawyers." So I tried sending out lawyer jokes for two weeks—and then I gave up.
>
> —Frustrated Entrepreneur

Informality is a leveling force. It provides an excellent context from which to let your talk flow out of the real you, not the manufactured one. It cuts away the stiffness and artificiality that bureaucracy can breed. It allows communication to be freer and less guarded, less political.

The Family Room

I have a pastor friend who offered to give me a tour of his church's new facility. I was glad to see it. It was very well appointed. Beautiful pastel green drapes went from ceiling to floor. Wall sconces were ubiquitous. The end result was lovely. As we stood in the back of the auditorium, we talked in hushed tones. There was no one else in the room. It just seemed like the thing to do (think funeral home here).

As he described the decorative influences that went into their choice of fabrics and colors, he said, "We wanted to have the auditorium feel like a living room." When he said the words *living room*, a lightbulb went on in my head. I had never thought of it before then, but I guess I had always wanted the decor at CTK to have the look and feel of the family room, not the living room. You know the difference, don't you? The living room is the room you keep clean, the room you use for company (so they think this is how well you keep the rest of your house). It's the room where you cannot put your feet up on the furniture or set down your drink without a coaster. It's the room where you put your best foot forward. It's the facade.

The family room, on the other hand, is where you *really* live. It's where magazines and newspapers are piled on the floor. It's where you can eat while you watch television. It's where Dad goes to snore in his recliner. It's where even the dog can curl up on the couch if he wants to. It is a homier, more relaxed environment.

The couch is a little worn. There are "mug rings" on the coffee table. Low on pretense, high on comfort.

At Christ the King our preference is not to meet in a church building. We find that the architecture itself can be a psychological barrier to the welcoming environment we are trying to create. We much prefer public spaces, where people already congregate for other reasons. Consider, for instance, the places where CTK has conducted worship services:

- Lodge hall
- Convention center
- Warehouse
- Cafeteria
- Gymnasium
- Roller rink
- Restaurant
- Coffee shop
- Barn
- City park
- Tulip field
- Amphitheater
- Beach
- Senior center
- Hotel conference room
- Swimming pool
- Fairground
- State park
- Performing arts center

Since these are places where unchurched people may already feel comfortable, we don't have to work so hard to help them feel at home.

Many churches think living room instead of family room and send out the vibe, "Fake it 'til you make it." In a Deliberately Simple church, we work hard to maintain a comfortable atmosphere.

We encourage people to make themselves at home. We think family room when it comes to the places we meet and even the colors and styles we employ.

A Deliberately Simple church takes a very utilitarian view of facilities and their appointments. A building is just a tool. It is not the church. The people are the church. We could meet under a tree and still be the church. (In fact, one of our CTK congregations in Pretoria, South Africa, does convene under a large tree.) The building, if we use one, is not our focal point. The people are. For this reason, we don't like to call the primary meeting place a sanctuary. We say, "auditorium" or "meeting room." We deinstitutionalize the facility. We want our facilities to be neat, clean, and functional and nothing else. What is special is not the place. What is special is what happens in the place. We don't use a pulpit. A music stand will do. We don't need fancy, just functional. By making it clear that we are not fixated on the surroundings, we help to reinforce that this is really about people.

What sorts of fixtures in a church might create a barrier for the people we are trying to reach?

One year at CTK we had the idea that we would have a Super Bowl party at the church, so men could watch the game together. The event came off okay, but afterward we gave it more thought and realized that Super Bowl Sunday is the biggest "small group day" of the year. Why would we want to take men out of their natural habitat and away from their friends when they could use the Super Bowl as a way to develop relationships with unchurched people?

Your Sunday Best

It is the value of reality that leads a Deliberately Simple church to encourage casual, comfortable dress. I always wear blue jeans to church. I do this because the average person in America owns eight pairs of blue jeans, so I consider them to be the least common denominator of fashion. The fashion statement (or understatement) that I make communicates something beyond the rivets and five pockets. It says, "We're not here to impress you, so please don't waste any effort trying to impress us."

Casual dress is not superficial; it's important. It's about being true to yourself and your ideas. We have neither the time nor the inclination for pretense. When clothing is allowed to convey class status within an organization, a hierarchical structure built on rank and position is perpetuated.

In the real estate industry, colored jackets have become a source of distinction among agencies, and amusement among those who don't have to wear them. At Red Carpet the jackets are red. At Century 21 they are gold. At ERA they are blue. RE/MAX, with its "let's keep it real" culture, ran an ad showing a male real estate agent in a sharp tailored suit and a female real estate agent in a luxurious fur coat, with the slogan, "These are our jackets." In a similar way, we at CTK have run an ad showing three young adults in jeans and T-shirts that says, "Put on your Sunday best. It's not a fashion show. It's just church."

While casual dress is encouraged at CTK, we do not have a reverse dress code. You can wear what you feel comfortable in. For some people, normal is a dress or a suit. That's fine. Wear what works for you. The point is that you don't have to dress up special for us, and you don't have to dress up special for God. Come as you are.

Blue jeans happen to be my answer to the question, "What do I normally wear?" so I've become well known for wearing jeans on Sunday as well. How important to people is my example of informality? Evidently, very. An anonymous poem was placed in the offering bucket at CTK, entitled "The Pastor in Blue Jeans."

For me the church has always been
A very important place to be.
But most of all, it's the relationship
Between my Jesus and me.

I'd often sit in uncomfortable pews
And experience rather boring scenes.
But then I found teaching so clear,
Given by a pastor in blue jeans.

Time and money and talents and gifts,
Given freely, but seemingly blown.
Only to have past efforts wasted
By churches that only cared for their own.

But now I've found a place that cares
For those who don't know what it means,
To put our hope in Jesus,
Lead by a pastor in blue jeans.

It's now easy to ask friends to come
With relevant teaching and worship is fun.
We're not trying to do everything,
Just the things that God has begun.

We're really all in this together.
And by thinking small, it seems,
We'll grow into God's special unit,
Captained by the pastor in blue jeans.

I have had dozens of conversations with unchurched people in which they bemoaned the fact that they didn't have anything to wear to church or quizzed me about what they should wear. They were surprised and relieved when I said, "Wear what you have on. You'll fit right in."

In a Deliberately Simple church, it's not a fashion show; it's a gathering of real people to have a real relationship with God.

Understated Liturgy

The services of a Deliberately Simple church are not lofty; they don't have a lot of fluff. Straightforward messages are given in a normal tone of voice and in conversational style. By staging our services loosely, we allow them to unfold with an edge of spontaneity. There is an opportunity for questions to be asked. Instead of running everything through the filter of religious subculture, we make an attempt to express ourselves normally and naturally.

> Formality suppresses dialogue; informality encourages it. Formal conversations leave little room for debate. They suggest that everything is scripted and predetermined. Informal dialogue is open. It invites questions, encouraging spontaneity and critical thinking.
>
> —Larry Bossidy, *Execution*

The minute the church starts to feel like a marketing campaign—more like a slogan than a reality—it begins to stray from reality. Deliberate Simplicity calls for an understated approach. No hard sell. A relative lack of hype. No over-the-top prognosticating. A conversational tenor. Better to understate our own importance or success so people can remember Who is truly important.

REAL PEOPLE ARE THE MINISTERS

When Jesus came to start his church, he did not pick twelve religious leaders to change the world. So how would Jesus start a church today? Would he raise half a million dollars, find a dynamic speaker, a worship leader, and a children's pastor, do a demographic study, secure a ministry campus, and saturate his community with a direct-mail campaign? Perhaps, but it is not how he did it the last time. Jesus simply took a dozen ordinary people, poured his life into them, and they became the church.

Those twelve were some of the 120 people who were filled with the Holy Spirit and began to spread the message of Jesus everywhere they went. Churches grew up wherever the gospel seed was planted. Church leaders gathered to brainstorm not how to grow the church but how to keep up with the growth of the church.

The book of Acts gives examples of nonprofessional pastors (Stephen, Philip, Aquila, Priscilla, etc.) doing extraordinary things to move the mission forward. Perhaps the most powerful example is found in Acts 8, when persecution scattered the church in Jerusalem throughout Judea and Samaria. Do you know what happened? Wherever these Jesus followers ended up, churches sprang up.

> The conventional church has become so complicated and difficult to pull off that only a rare person who is a professional can do it every week.... When church is so complicated, its function is taken out of the hands of the common Christian and placed in the hands of a few talented professionals. This results in a passive church whose members come and act more like spectators than empowered agents of God's Kingdom.
>
> —Neil Cole, *Organic Church*

God does not need superstars in order to advance his kingdom. Real people will do. A realistic approach delivers us from the "great man of God" theory. This is a faulty understanding of how God works in people's lives. It creates an unhealthy relationship between leaders and followers. The leader is cast as the one through whom God will primarily work, thus creating a "bigger than life" image. Because of the special call of God on the leader, his actions are above question. This approach overlooks the biblical fact that while God has given us different gifts and roles, he intends to use every person, and we are all members of the same body.

> In past spiritual awakenings, dynamic preachers went into society to bring people into a local church for further development. This era of spiritual growth is different. It features millions of individuals quietly using the weapons of faith that God has given them to be scions of transformation within the framework of their typical space and

> connections. The starting point is internal, not external; the message is their own transformation by Christ, made real in their words and deeds.
>
> —George Barna, *Revolution*

At CTK we see real people as the ministers. As a sign posted on a university bulletin board once had it, "No gurus is good gurus." Every man, woman, boy, and girl has been created with ministry potential. Ministry does not require a great man, a great call, or a great gift. The man or woman God uses is common. God gives to every one of his children the permission to lead others to Christ. A friend once wrote me a great compliment: "Thank you for showing me that a real man can be less than perfect. Thank you for being extraordinarily ordinary." I think I know now what I want on my tombstone.

Neil Cole is the founder of Church Multiplication Associates, an organization that has started hundreds of smaller house churches. While visiting one of the groups, he told them he thought Satan was more worried about their minichurch than about the megachurch in town. The group participants laughed, but Neil explained himself by asking, "How many of you could go out and start a church like one of those megachurches?" None of the group members raised their hands. "Okay, how many of you could start a church like this one?" They all raised their hands. Neil concluded, "I assure you, Satan is terrified by this."

Francis Shaeffer said, "No little people and no little places." Every believer is called into ministry. If God has saved you, he has saved you for a purpose. Some have greater gifts than others. But every believer is equipped to do God's work. Ministry is simply meeting people where they are, with what they need, to get where they need to go.

> You can do what I cannot do. I can do what you cannot do. Together we can do great things.
>
> —Mother Teresa

In an organic construct, the pastor's role is to create and sustain an environment wherein the people of the church can carry out their ministry with minimal obstacles and maximum fulfillment. He is not so much to do the ministry as to see that the ministry gets done.

> [Christ] gave some to be … pastors and teachers, to prepare God's people for works of service, so that the body of Christ may be built up until we all reach unity in the faith and in the knowledge of the Son of God and become mature, attaining to the whole measure of the fullness of Christ.
>
> —Ephesians 4:11–13

If a church orients its ministry around its pastor, it loses its groundedness. In a church oriented around professional ministry, attenders tend to be passive observers, while professional ministers tend to be overworked. It's not God's method. From the Scriptures we get a philosophy, and from that philosophy we get a methodology: the pastors are to prepare God's people for works of service. As a pastor moves toward a "prepare the real ministers" style of ministry, he moves toward greater effectiveness.

what might keep a pastor doing the ministry himself instead of seeing that the ministry gets done?

In this model, the pastor gets to come down off his pedestal and be a real person too. The pastor, like the others, wears an ingredients label that reads, "Dust and Divine Spit." He is made out of the same stuff and faces the same life issues. He has an important role, but he is not on a different level. He is free to be who he is in Christ. The weight of the church is not on his shoulders alone. When every believer is a minister, it creates a healthier body.

Jesus intended not to build a religious organization but to start a movement of real people to transform the spiritual landscape. Religious people and systems have always made things complicated for God. Religious institutions trend toward conformity and control. Instead of empowering people, they enslave them.

While some church movements found their impetus in special revelation, the Deliberate Simplicity movement is grounded in common sense. Common sense is also a gift from God; it's just widely distributed. And maybe because it is so common, it is not esteemed (familiarity breeds contempt). Deliberate Simplicity celebrates commonsense solutions.

In 1971, when Southwest Airlines appeared on the scene, they began issuing a ticket that resembled a bus ticket. The only problem was that passengers would often throw out the ticket with other receipts in their pocket. Southwest had meetings to discuss a solution, and there was a proposal put forth for a multimillion dollar computerized ticketing system. During the discussion, a vice president came up with an alternate, low-tech solution. He suggested printing across the ticket, on both ends, "THIS IS A TICKET." Southwest tried it, and it worked!

> State a moral case to a ploughman and a professor. The former will decide it as well and often better than the latter because he has not been led astray by artificial rules.
>
> —Thomas Jefferson

Jeff Bezos of Amazon.com believes in the power of being "simpleminded." In the face of complex choices, he relies primarily on common sense about what would be in the best interests of his customers.

One night Sherlock Holmes and Dr. Watson went camping. In the middle of the night, Holmes woke up and saw the stars shining above him. He called out to Watson, "What does seeing the stars in the middle of the night mean to you?" Watson awoke and gazed at the sky and then said, "Infinity is sometimes incomprehensible and sometimes comprehensible. We are but a speck in the universe, yet we are blessed with a thing called consciousness...." "Watson, you idiot," interrupted Holmes, "it means that someone stole our tent."

I fear that the modern church is more like Watson than Holmes. We have turned church growth into a science. We have extensive rationalizations and permutations. We have demographic studies. We know our parking ratios. We have theories of ingress and egress. But we are missing out on the simple, relational aspects of ministry that are life-changing.

Christianity is not a religion; it's a lifestyle. It's the difference between attending a car show and being in the automobile garage with the hood up. Christ came to set us free to work on our stuff. The protocol, tradition, formalities, and observances of religious systems get in the way of the work we need to do.

> The church culture has been confused with biblical Christianity, both inside the church and out. In reality, the church culture in North America is a vestige of the original movement, an institutional expression of religion that is in part a civil religion and in part a club where religious people can hang out with other people whose politics, worldview and lifestyle match theirs. As he hung on the cross Jesus probably never thought the impact of his sacrifice would be reduced to an invitation for people to join and support an institution.
>
> —Reggie McNeal, *The Present Future*

Jesus did not die on the cross to fill church auditoriums, to enable magnificent church campuses to be funded, or to motivate people to implement innovative programs. He died because He loves you and me, He wants an everlasting

> relationship with us, and He expects that connection with us to be so all-consuming that we become wholly transformed—Jesus clones, if you will indulge the expression.
>
> —George Barna, *Revolution*

In response to religiosity, the first thing we need is a dynamic, authentic relationship with Jesus Christ. The last thing we need is any substitute.

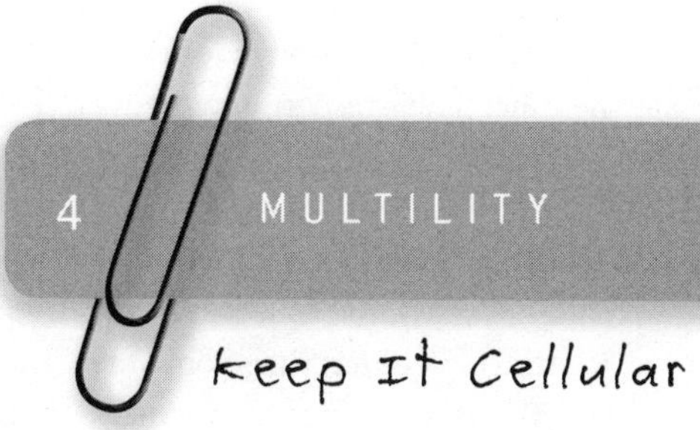

WHAT IF . . .

Back and Forth

In the mid-1990s Christ the King Community Church in Bellingham clustered in five services (of a few hundred people) on two campuses. One was its original site, a smaller church building in Laurel, Washington, about ten miles north of Bellingham. The other was a converted warehouse on the north edge of town. For a couple years we held services at both locations and staggered the start times in forty-five-minute intervals to allow for drive time between the locations. So a service would start at 8:30 at the Bellingham campus, with a service at the Laurel campus starting at 9:15, to be followed by a 10:00 service in Bellingham, and so forth. We had five services each Sunday morning between the two campuses. You would preach in one place, go out the back door, get in your car, and drive quickly to the other location. It was a chaotic, crazy, exhilarating time. But people were being led to Christ and baptized. The church was growing rapidly. It defied explanation. It was a God thing.

As we reached capacity, I put forward another proposal. "What if"—words you often hear from me—"we started a third location?"

It seemed like a really crazy idea to the pastors and leaders of CTK at the time. Their response to me was, "Don't you see how out of control this is?" It appeared that they thought *out of control* were bad words. I was quite comfortable with them. But the leaders of CTK at that time felt we should move toward consolidation of our activities. Clearly, the time was not right for the idea God had put on my heart: a church that would meet in many locations. When in 1997 Christ the King Community Church purchased an eighty-thousand-square-foot building on the north side of Bellingham, I was excited. After all, we would obviously be the largest church in the area, and that would feel like success.

Before and After

In 1998 CTK in Bellingham consolidated on one larger campus as a megachurch. I had a front-row seat for the switch from two locations to one location. But when we moved in, I realized we had lost something in the transition, something we could not get back.

Overnight we went from convening people by hundreds at a time in several services to convening them by thousands at a time in a couple of services. On a certain level, people were excited to realize that we had "arrived." But on another level, there was a hollow feeling of being a crowd instead of a community. The difference between a community and a crowd is connection. If you get a bunch of people in the same room who have no connection to each other, you have a crowd. If you get a bunch of people in the same room who are connected to each other, you have a community. It is through community that we have our needs met and are able to meet the needs of others. It is through community that the church can be the church.

Prior to the consolidation, our small group assimilation system consisted of people looking across the room, identifying someone as new in the environment, walking over to them, and asking, "Are you in a small group yet? Would you like to come to ours?" It was as simple, direct, and powerful as that. Once we began convening in a huge auditorium, nearly all this grassroots behavior ceased. Instead, the pastoral team would meet on Tuesday with a list of individuals who wanted to be in a small group. We would read through the names, asking, "Does anyone know the Smiths? How about the Joneses?" After shaking our heads, we would set about trying to hook up people we didn't know with people they didn't know who didn't know them. It was a laborious, inefficient, ineffective system.

After we moved into the large building, our once-robust double-digit growth rate slowed to low single digits. One factor limiting growth: space limitations. Ironic, huh?

I had dreamed of pastoring a megachurch for years, but when it finally happened, it didn't feel like progress to me. The unique way in which I got to see it happen (meeting in smaller groups one week, in a large group the next) created a vivid "before and after" picture of the trade-offs that come with increased scale. The experience inspired me to explore ways to propagate clusters instead of moving de facto toward the "bigger is better" paradigm.

A CHURCH DISTRIBUTED

In 1999, through a series of God-directed events, I was able to implement a Deliberately Simple approach to church development with the founding of Christ the King Community Church of Skagit Valley, Washington. I told the core group that gathered then, "We're not going to ask everyone to come to us. We're going to ask us to go to them." They all nodded their heads in agreement, but I doubt they knew what I was talking about. I didn't even know what I was talking about. I just knew I wanted to find out what was down the road we hadn't taken in Bellingham. I had a dream of a church that would multiply from one to two to three sites, and maybe beyond. I said, "We want to reach an unlimited number of people in an unlimited number of places." In a few years, to my surprise and delight, this church expanded into other counties, states, and countries and changed its name to Christ the King Community Church, International.

A Hewlett-Packard television commercial pictures a man in a single scull, rowing smoothly through pristine water. All of a sudden his face lights up. The next scene shows him at a pay phone on the dock, saying excitedly, "Bill, what if . . ." And then his voice trails off. The commercial ends with a voice-over and a logo, aligning the advertised company with creative thinking and innovation. The commercial is memorable because I resonate with the question, what if? Those two words fire up my imagination. They stimulate my passion.

- What if a church became more outward focused than inward focused?
- What if, when a church outgrew its location, it started up in an additional location instead of building a bigger building?
- What if a church grew in an unlimited way—by multiplication instead of addition?
- What if a church took the resources it had been allocating toward buildings and put them into leader development?
- What if a church could aspire to become a movement instead of a ministry?

As I have reflected on these questions, a vision for the church has crystallized in my mind. (To say that I caught a vision for the church would be incorrect. It would be better to say that a vision for the church caught me.) It is a vision of a church growing exponentially, by multiplying believers, leaders, groups, services, and sites. It is a church characterized by multility.

> **mul•til•i•ty** *n*: a commitment to multiples of some thing, instead of a larger version of that thing

Multility contends that more is better than bigger. Multility is growth by cell division, the replicating model of organic systems. Organic systems are implicitly self-sustaining and reproducible.

They multiply through germination, reproduction, and mitosis. Can the church grow that way?

Do You Want Fries with That?

I was first intrigued with multility as a child. A new fast-food restaurant came to my hometown of Anchorage, Alaska. There were big yellow arches out front. They had a clown named Ronald. But what startled me most was the sign. Right from the start, they had a reader board that said, "40 million served." I remember thinking, "Wow, how did they do that?" My parents filled me in: "Son, they are a chain, which means that they have restaurants in lots of different places. That's how they did that." I thought that was a cool idea. Evidently, McDonald's was faced with a choice when they reached capacity: either build a bigger restaurant to serve more people or build more restaurants to serve more people. They went the more restaurant route. The rest, as they say, is history (they are now approaching 100 billion served).

Of course, banks, grocery stores, hospitals, and universities have also taken a multisite strategy, with good effect. In his book *Discontinuity and Hope*, church consultant Lyle Schaller describes the possibilities for a church to expand into multiple locations. He contrasts a longtime resident showing an old friend around town in 1965 and 2002.

> **1965**: "That's the First National Bank at the corner of Main and Washington, and directly across from it is First Church, where we have been members since we moved here thirty years ago. The college is four blocks to the east up on the hill, our hospital is about a half mile to the west, and our doctor has his office in that building over there."
>
> **2002**: "That's the First National Bank, but I haven't been there for years. We do all our banking at a branch supermarket where we buy groceries. We're members of First Church, but we go to their east-side campus, which is within walking distance of our house. We have one

congregation, one staff, one budget, and one treasury, but three meeting places—a small one on the north side of town, the big one out where we live, and the old building downtown here. The old college up on the hill is now a university. This is their main campus, but they also offer classes at three other locations. We're members of an HMO that has doctors in five locations, but my primary-care physician is in a branch about a mile from where we live. Her office is next to a branch of the main hospital, so I've never been in the main hospital except to visit a couple of friends. Our older daughter is enrolled in a theological school out in California, but she is able to take all her classes on the east-side campus of First Church. That enables her to live with us and saves her a lot of money. We also look after her two children while she's in class or in the library."[10]

Of all the entities that could benefit from multiple locations, I believe the church should be first in line.

Childhood Dreams

My positive notions of multility were reinforced in Sunday school when I came to realize that the New Testament church did not meet in a church building. In fact, they did not meet in one place at all, but instead gathered in private homes ("house to house") and public spaces ("the temple courts"). With childlike wonder, I dreamed of what might happen if a church were to try that again.

After accepting Christ at an early age, I began preparing for the ministry. Throughout my teen years, the model of success I observed was the megachurch. This was in the midseventies, when churches of one thousand to two thousand or more people began to spring up across the country. As I drank at the well of "bigger is better," I quickly lost my childhood fantasies of a church meeting in small groups and gathering in public places. In Bible college and seminary I investigated church growth theory in earnest. Following completion of seminary, I pastored two denominational churches and quickly started to climb the ladder of success.

> Bigger is better turned out to be another twentieth-century myth.
>
> —Peter Drucker

In my first full-time pastorate, as the church was growing rapidly around me, there was also a growing discontent within me. I was working harder and harder, with diminishing returns. Attendance and expectations were growing, but I was not. The church was program driven. The pressure was intense. In quiet moments I flashed back to the simple ideas I had of the church as a child. Eventually the disconnect between my childhood dream and my adult reality grew to a point of personal crisis.

In the early nineties I made a radical proposal to the traditional church I was pastoring. I suggested that we drop the denominational name of the church and prepare to launch a second location in a town ten minutes to the north. It was clearly a watershed, make-or-break proposal. Truly, we would be putting everything at risk for the cause. The stakes were high, especially for the stakeholders. For such a significant change, the constitution of the church called for a two-thirds positive vote of the membership. I pushed hard, but the system pushed back. When the moment of truth arrived (we needed a two-thirds vote), it failed to pass by one vote. It was the death of a vision. Intense discouragement set in. I left that church, and the ministry for that matter, about a year later.

Eventually I found myself on the back row of Christ the King Community Church in Bellingham, Washington, a church that has taken some significant steps in small group and multicampus ministry. It has given me the freedom to press the model even further through church planting. I can see now that this is God's plan for my life.

The Goal . . . the Prize

Paul recognized a vision for his life and ministry, a vision that released energy and focus. He said, "I press on toward the goal to win the prize for which God has called me heavenward in Christ Jesus" (Phil. 3:14). In other words, Paul says, "I have a goal . . . to win the prize." Some might think that the prize is heaven. But the prize isn't heaven. The prize relates to heaven, but the prize is here and now. In an earlier verse, Paul says in effect, "I haven't attained it yet . . . that's why I'm pressing on." The sense is that he'll attain it not in the next life but in this one. The sense is that he's in the locker room at halftime and the game's not over yet. This contest is still to be decided on the field, and he's giving himself a pep talk: "Go out there and reach that goal and win that prize!"

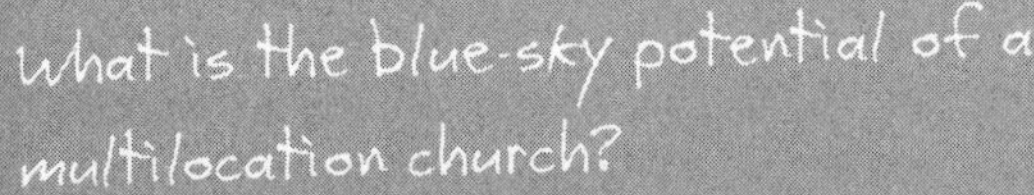

For a Deliberately Simple church, the prize is to see the propagation of Christ's kingdom through the multiplication of small groups and worship centers. The reward is a church that spreads like wildfire. The trophy is large numbers of lost people coming to salvation.

One of the key questions any growth-oriented leader must answer is, "If we are successful in fulfilling our mission, and we effectively reach out, how will we be able to accommodate growing numbers of converts?" Answers to this question could run down two tracks: bigger or more. We either find a bigger container to hold more people or find more containers to hold more people. That is, if a church were to grow from one hundred to one thousand people, structurally it could look two different ways.

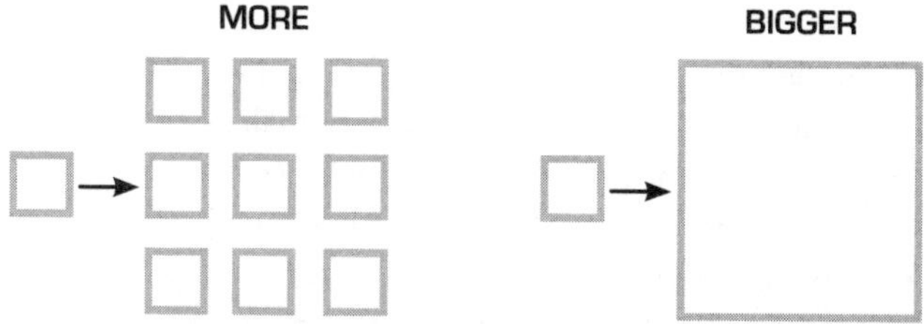

Success, as it is defined by most of Christianity, is counter to reproduction. But in a Deliberately Simple church, we don't think bigger is necessarily better. We think more is better. "Is it better to be big or small?" James O'Toole asks. "Obviously, it is best to be both at the same time."

Other social organizations have found benefit in self-imposed size limitations, with replication and relationship. Bill Gross is one of the leaders of a Hutterite community outside of Spokane, Washington. He explains the natural process that starts to take place when people begin to become strangers to each other: "What happens when you get that big is that the group starts, just on its own, to form a sort of clan. You get two or three groups within the larger group. That is something you really try to prevent, and when it happens it is a good time to branch out."

Bill Gore, founder of the company that makes Gore-Tex, is committed to multility for his workforce. He limits the size of his plants to not more than 150 employees (a size he feels is optimum for a sense of family). To insure this size, he limits the parking lost size to 150 cars. He knows it is time to build a new plant when employees start parking on the grass.

Over the years, military planners have arrived at a rule of thumb which dictates that functional fighting units cannot be substantially larger than two hundred soldiers. When they get larger than that, people become strangers to each other. You have to impose more hierarchies, rules and regulations, and formal measures to try to command loyalty and cohesion. When fighting units are smaller than that, orders can be implemented and unruly behavior controlled informally, on the basis of personal interaction.

Some ministries of the church, such as small group ministries, have leveraged the principle of multility for quite a while. Small group proponents have said for years that the fastest way for a church to begin growing by 10 percent annually is to break the church into groups of ten and have every small group reach out to one new person each year. In other words, on a micro instead of macro scale, more people get involved in the mission.

Deliberate Simplicity contends that in the same way, distributed growth works on a churchwide level. Through multiple services and sites, a church is able to distribute the responsibility for outreach. For instance, by having three services, if each service reaches out to ten new people this year, the church will grow by thirty, and yet ten new people is really very attainable for each of the services. And by having ten locations, if each grows by thirty people over the next year, the church grows by nearly three hundred people. Growing by three hundred people a year might seem like a challenge for a church that meets in one place at one time.

The growth model of McDonald's is more instead of bigger. McDonald's replicates itself at a certain size as many times as necessary to serve a population center. In a major city, there may be dozens or even hundreds of McDonald's restaurants. It's even possible for there to be two just down the street from each other. McDonald's has found an optimum size for their objectives. Instead of thinking bigger to accommodate more people, they think more.

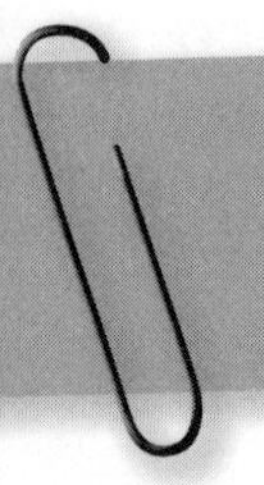

How does an experience at a big-box retailer differ from an experience at McDonald's?

Scale and Reciprocity

Bigness and fame go together like peanut butter and jelly. They have to. Small systems can be conversational and egalitarian. Large systems must revert to a broadcast paradigm. Broadcast television is the perfect embodiment of the one-way nature of fame, but megachurches are also of that ilk. People know you, but you don't know them. Sociologist Clay Shirky describes fame as "an extreme imbalance between inbound and outbound attention. Two things are required to create this inequity: scale and reciprocity. To be famous, you need to receive a minimal amount of attention from an audience of at least thousands."

Arguably the most influential American Christian leader of modern times has been Billy Graham. Billy came on the scene in the 1960s, as modern broadcast methods were hitting their stride. He was able to capitalize on the state of the culture at that time. Broadcasting was en vogue (stadium events, television, etc.). The leadership model was the "great man" model. It was fitting for Billy to leverage the elements of the culture that were available to him. Billy has certainly been successful utilizing the broadcast model. Megachurches have piggybacked on this model in the past couple decades. They are regional. They are massive. The theory: the bigger the building, the more people you can reach. The megachurch mirrors the big-box retailer. The Deliberately Simple church mirrors a restaurant chain.

> How can you create a small-company environment and still continue to grow and prosper? The answer is the network corporation, and the facilitator is technology. Technology breaks down barriers that block the door to the next generation corporate environment. Networked computers, sophisticated but affordable communications capabilities, and strategic use of information systems suddenly create a myriad of possibilities.
>
> —Pat McGovern, *Chief Executive*, April 1990

If the next generation of evangelists is to be successful, we will need to leverage the technologies and mentalities that are available to us, such as the internet and clusters.

PLURALITY OF MINISTRIES

At CTK we want to encourage multility at every level. One application of multility is to the ministries in which a church may engage. For instance, we prefer the word *ministries* (plural) instead of *ministry* (singular). This allows for diversity and innovation and multiplies the opportunities we have to reach out. So we don't have a women's ministry; we have women's ministries. We don't have a youth ministry; we have youth ministries, etc. We don't imagine that any one ministry can meet the needs.

While there are a limited number of programs that a Deliberately Simple church may initiate (see chapter 1, "Minimality"), there are an unlimited number of ministries that individuals may initiate. While corporate programs are discouraged, individual ministries are encouraged.

Ministries Instead of Programs

Deliberate Simplicity makes a distinction between a program and a ministry. The difference between the two is that programs

Programs	Ministries
Centralized	Decentralized
Corporate	Individual
Top-down	Bottom-up
Singular	Plural
Perpetual	Temporary

are centralized, corporate, top-down, singular, and perpetual. Ministries are decentralized, individual, bottom-up, plural, and temporary.

An example of a church program might be a midweek children's program. The program is centralized, in that everyone comes to the church to participate. The program is corporate, because it is sponsored and directed by the church organization. It is top-down, in that the impetus for the program comes from the pastor or staff. It is singular, because it is the only program of its kind that the church backs. It is perpetual, since the program has been going for years and will likely continue to do so.

On the other hand, imagine an after-school girls' group that meets midweek. The program is decentralized, as the group does not necessarily need to meet at a church facility. It is personal, because the initiation and facilitation of the group has come from a mother of one of the girls. It is bottom-up, since the idea for this ministry did not come from the church's leadership. It is plural, because many of these groups could conceivably meet in various homes. It is temporary, since the ministry will no longer exist if the parents who lead it choose to discontinue.

Empower Instead of Control

At Christ the King we don't like the word *control*. We like the word *empower*. Authoritarian cultures spawn passivity and create codependency. To combat that tendency, we train people in our organization to be ready and able to say, "Yes, sure, you bet." Often, those are words that cannot be spoken in church. As is typical in a bureaucracy, church leaders tend to have the power to say no but seldom have the power to say yes. We want yes to be a valid answer again in the church. God is at work in people's lives. We want to unleash the church.

While corporately we do not initiate a lot of ministries (we stay focused on the priorities of small groups, worship, and outreach), many ministries emerge because we empower volunteers to do what God is calling them to do. CTK serves as an umbrella under which individual ministries can flourish.

In our context, the role of the pastors and staff is to create and sustain an environment where the people of the church (the real ministers) can carry out their ministries with minimum obstacles and maximum fulfillment. The paid staff is focused on climate control. In other words, they manage the conditions of the system but not necessarily the behavior.

A few years ago a lady came to me with a heart to reach out at Thanksgiving time to people who have no place to go to share a holiday meal. I told her to go for it. She put together a group of friends to organize the event, solicited area businesses for donations, recruited cooks and waiters, and now has developed an annual ministry that reaches hundreds of people each Thanksgiving eve. She had no previous experience doing this. We shouted encouragement and gave her a little bit of coaching from the sidelines, but basically the event was her baby. Her baby ended up being a major outreach involving corporate sponsors, professional chefs, musicians, and a huge volunteer crew. This sort of story has been repeated hundreds of times in other places. It is amazing what ordinary people can do when we get out of their way. Our culture of empowerment makes it possible for dreams to become reality. We have the faith to say yes to God's leading in a person's life.

Prosumers Instead of Consumers

In a Deliberately Simple church, we ask the people who attend to be prosumers instead of consumers. The word *prosumer* was coined by futurist Alvin Toffler to describe the psyche of a participant who actively contributes to the experience he or she is enjoying (as opposed to a consumer, who consumes the experience). With a pro(+)sumer, there is more of "it" after the individual has interacted with it. With a con(-)sumer, there is less of "it" after the individual has interacted with it.

The ministry structure at a Deliberately Simple church is analogous to a picnic at a park. The church organization rents the park gazebo and provides the hamburgers and hot dogs. But the people coming to the picnic have to bring the rest—salads, desserts, and games. The basics of community and worship are supplied by the organization. But individual ministries provide flavor and variety to the ministry. Because the church encourages individual ministries instead of corporate programs, people bring a healthy variety of skills, passions, insights, and relationships to the party.

Yes Instead of No

The first page of the operating agreement of the Great Harvest Bread Company is emblazoned with big, bold letters that state, "Anything not expressly prohibited by the language of this agreement *is allowed*."

When it comes to supporting individual ministry, there are four words in which every Deliberately Simple pastor needs to become fluent. These four words are, "Yes, sure, you bet." "Yes," "Sure," and "You bet" need to be spoken frequently to make certain that we are open to God's plans, not just our own—to guarantee that we are empowering people instead of controlling them.

Over the years, I have been amazed at how powerful these words have been to the hearer. Evidently, they are rarely spoken (or heard) in the traditional church anymore.

At CTK we value empowerment. We want to have faith not only in God but also in people. That means saying yes to what God wants to do in a person's life. While there are a limited number of programs that we start, there are an unlimited number of ministries that our people may start. There are a number of people in ministry at CTK who have told me, "I couldn't do this at my previous church. There was too much red tape."

In modern church circles, a barrier to ministry is often excellence. What this means to many people is that those who are average need not apply. At CTK we emphasize good enough instead of perfection. This opens the door to many people who previously would not have been considered gifted enough to minister.

We allow people to minister even after they have failed or fallen. We believe that "hope for the future, forgiveness for the past" applies to everyone, even leaders. A church leader from another denomination told me recently that the difference between their group and CTK was that we actually give a person a second chance. His denomination talked the language of recovery but fell short on actually taking a risk. We take the risk.

Decentralized Instead of Centralized

Multilocation ministry calls for a decentralized organizational architecture and new language. At CTK we have chosen to call each congregation a worship center. Technically, there is only one church—the sum of all the small groups and worship centers.

The organizational philosophy of CTK resembles fingers reaching out instead of a clinched fist. Multility pushes out the cellular and congregational functions of the church, while the traditional church centralizes its services and groups.

The big idea of multility is to convene different worship services, at different times, in different locations, with different worship teams, and with different preachers. Each of these venues is a manifestation of the larger body.

Is there anything wrong with the centralized model? No. We just believe that God has called us to try something different. While the megachurch has become good at being big and centralized, we are trying to become good at being small and decentralized. We are both trying to reach large numbers of people, just in different ways.

More Instead of Bigger

God desires for his church to grow numerically as well as spiritually. Bob Jones, founder of the conservative university that bears

CENTRALIZED CHURCH MINISTRY

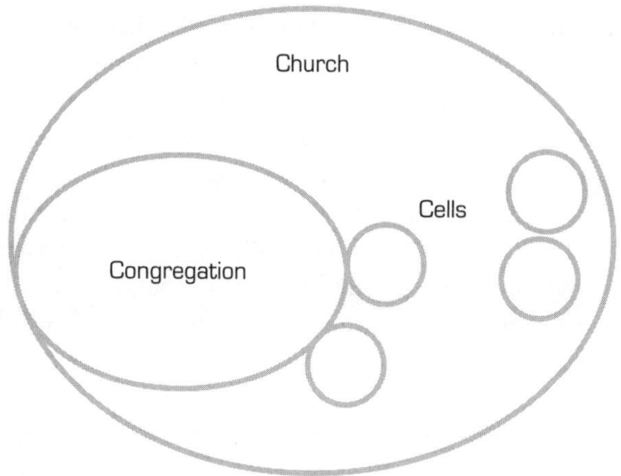

DECENTRALIZED CHURCH MOVEMENT

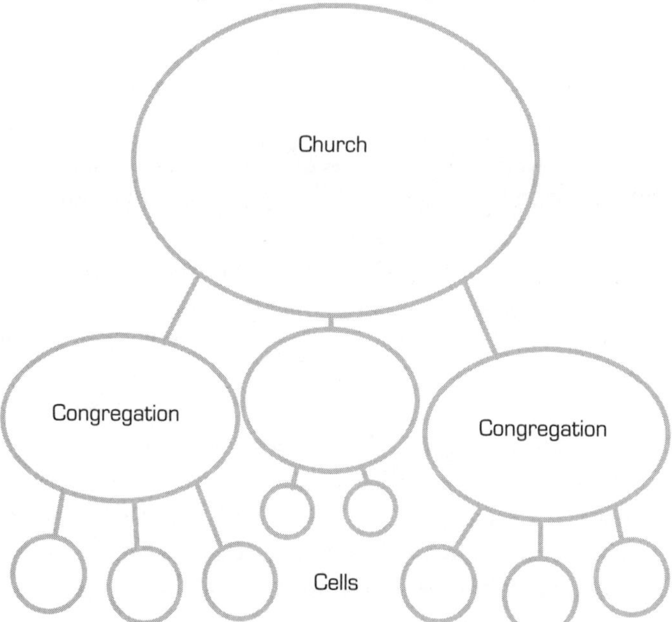

his name, once said, "Jesus promised that 'where two or three are gathered, there am I in the midst of them,' but that doesn't mean that he doesn't like a bigger crowd." I happen to agree with Jones on this point. What indicators do we have that Jesus would like a bigger crowd? Peter's commentary: "The Lord ... is patient with you, not wanting anyone to perish, but everyone to come to repentance" (2 Peter 3:9). Paul's commentary: "The whole body ... grows as God causes it to grow" (Col. 2:19). God's command, related by Jesus in the parable of the great banquet: "Go out to the roads and country lanes and make them come in, so that my house will be full" (Luke 14:23).

Some may look at CTK, see that it is small pieces loosely joined, and conclude that we prefer small over big. We don't, actually. We prefer more over bigger. That is, we want to reach an unlimited number of people (more people than you could ever put in any one facility), but we feel that the best way to do this is to be in an unlimited number of places. This is our "theory of the business," what Peter Drucker described as the important work of defining the environment of the organization, where intellect and spirit align. For instance, Sam Walton, founder of Wal-Mart, articulated his theory of business with his famous declaration, "I will continue to reduce prices as long as I live." Our theory of business, where intellect and spirit align for us, is to be one church with many ministries, here, there, and everywhere. Individually, none of them may be that sizeable, but together they will present a formidable influence on the culture. This is what gives us our energy.

We feel that our calling is not to build a church but to reach a community. And we feel that trying to reach large numbers of people in one place is a very limited idea. So at CTK we feel we need to grow larger and smaller at the same time! We need to keep breaking it down so we can always make good on our pledge: "Always a place for you." The time to start a new location is when we have the leadership to execute it, rather than the people to attend it.

It's our job to cast the nets and God's job to fill them. What we've generally found is that when we step out in faith, the Lord responds with growth. Typically, we've seen significant growth in overall attendance as we add more services. Perhaps a rule of thumb might be that 80 percent capacity becomes 50 percent capacity twice when one service becomes two. In other words, if one service has eighty people meeting in an auditorium that seats one hundred, two services might have fifty each (including new people who come, old-timers who come back, etc.). So the church immediately grows by 20 percent and now is positioned to grow rapidly to two hundred people without anyone feeling more crowded than they were prior to the change. You do lose the thrill of having eighty people packed into the room each service, but you are giving that up for the ultimate thrill of reaching out to more people and growing Christ's kingdom.

It is clear that God wants his followers to reach an unlimited number of people. Did he give us any clues as to how we should do that? In Acts 1:8 Jesus says, "You will receive power when the Holy Spirit comes on you; and you will be my witnesses in Jerusalem, and in all Judea and Samaria, and to the ends of the earth." Note what he doesn't say here. He doesn't say, "You will have the biggest church you could imagine in Jerusalem. People will ride in on chariots from the surrounding communities."

How big God's church gets is his business. We just know we want to reach out to an unlimited number of people, or as many as we possibly can. The best way we know to do that is the way he suggested—by being in as many places as possible.

Throughout history, great moves of God have often accompanied a decentralized approach. John Wesley was a great revivalist. He also had his methods. As a student in Oxford, he became known as John Wesley, the Methodist. He placed people in small groups, as part of a society. The groups were to remain small but to help start new groups. He would send around traveling preachers and bands. It was a way to effectively reach out to and care for increasing numbers of people. In a five-year period, one hundred thousand people came to faith in Christ. It became a movement that transformed the spiritual landscape. I view Wesley's methodology to be the precursor to the Deliberate Simplicity movement.

NETWORKS WORK

Networks are the wave of the foreseeable future. They combine efficiency with effectiveness. The evolution from mainframe machines to the networked PC is one of the most significant cultural changes to happen in our lifetime. It forecasts the shift from the monolocation church to the multilocation church that is socially atomized.

Small Pieces Loosely Joined

The architectural paradigm shift of the internet—often referred to as "small pieces loosely joined"—is proving that it is more impacting to build large systems out of smaller functions which are separately packaged and interconnected. By operating in an interdependent way, the smaller pieces are able to participate in larger undertakings. It is the architecture of participation, where sharing increases value.

Networks that welcome irregular participation are replacing classes that called for regular attendance. Networks of like-minded people are replacing geographically defined congregations. Groups with similar missional goals are replacing denominations. This emerging era is characterized by the collaborative innovation of people working in community, just as innovation in the industrial era was characterized by individual genius.

Sharing is the primary benefit of a network. A network allows self-interested behavior to redound to the benefit of us all. As individuals create value for themselves, they make the group (the rest of us) smarter. Collaboration also guarantees a diversity of perspectives. In fact, a network of people with dissimilar knowledge is of far greater value than a network of people with the same ideas.

The internet is moving from sharing an experience to creating a shared experience. The transition is being powered by the bottom-up nature of sharing and collective action. It's exemplified by such developments as the barn-raising methodology of Wikipedia, open source P2P (peer-to-peer) systems, Wi-Fi, e-commerce sites such as Amazon and eBay, plus Google, RSS, and dozens of other dots that are being connected to fulfill the original promise of the net.

A multilocation church attempts to balance the ownership and pride that comes with autonomy with the synergy and impact that comes with cooperation. At Christ the King we call our organizational philosophy "Freedom with handrails." The handrails are our beliefs and our brand. Inside those two rails, we want individual parts to enjoy as much freedom as possible. Another analogy would be a necklace. There is a string that holds the beads together as part of a bigger whole. The string in the case of a multisite church is the church's mission, vision, and values. Each bead is independent but, by coordinating with other beads around a common mission, is able to experience a more meaningful existence than a bead could in isolation.

All for One, One for All

The Deliberately Simple church values interdependence over either dependence or independence. Most of us have very little experience working interdependently, as part of a network. The culture (churches included) has reinforced the Darwinian belief that the central fact of life is competition rather than cooperation. The motto of modernity is, "I've got mine" instead of "All for one, one for all."

Interdependence requires some things that independence does not. Specifically, it requires higher levels of trust, others-orientation, and communication. You cannot be distrusting, selfish, or isolated and function in an interdependent way. You must share fortune and misfortune. You must see the bigger picture. You must do your job but not forget about our job. You must think globally but act locally. You must work together separately.

> What's the biggest problem in the world of security today? Simple. The CIA won't talk to the FBI ... who won't talk to Customs ... who won't talk to the INS ... who won't talk to the Air Force ... who won't talk to the Army ... who won't talk to the Navy. (And the few who do choose to talk across walls are seen as "disloyal" to, say, "200 proud years" of Army or Navy tradition.) And so on. Fighting "virtual states" like Al Qaeda demands seamless (Big, Big Word) integration of our domestic and international security forces. In fact, integration of the civilized world's domestic and international security assets.
>
> —Tom Peters, *Re-Imagine*

John Briggs, in his book *Seven Life Lessons of Chaos*, describes the joy seen in sports when people work in concert with others: "One of the most exciting sports experiences anyone can have is watching a team catch fire. Perhaps as a basketball game begins, the players on one team seem to be operating independently of one another, mechanically going through their routines, in effect competing among themselves. Then they suddenly undergo a transformation. One of them makes an inspired play that leads to a basket: At this instant a bifurcation point becomes amplified. Now the moves the players make seem coupled together, all five team members working like a single organism."

Briggs's description of a team catching fire harks back to analogies the Scriptures use for the church. The Bible describes the church as a body with all the parts being necessary, or as living stones that together make up a spiritual house.

In the natural world, interdependence is the norm. Swarms, flocks, hives, colonies, pods, whoops, and flanges. Call them what you will, but many organisms live in social groups. Dennis Bakke, former CEO of AES and author of *Joy at Work*, based his honeycomb organizational structure on remembrances from his childhood farm, specifically the pattern of bees working together to collect nectar. Even the structure of the honeycomb they were working on was illustrative.

One supercolony of ants discovered in Japan is estimated to be home to 407 million red wood ants. The giant network is made up of 45,000 smaller colonies and ruled by over 1 million queens. The colony stretches for thirteen miles and may have begun over one thousand years ago.

In nature, there is clearly a preference for the horizontal, spiral (connect and collaborate) creation model instead of the vertical (command and control), top-down creation model. In the vertical model the key word is *contain*, while in the horizontal model the word to use is *involve*.

California redwood trees are known to be some of the largest trees in the world. The secret of their ability to stand tall is not in their deep root system. The secret is in the fact that the roots of the trees are interconnected with the roots of the trees growing around them. They are interdependent. Each one needs the others.

Together, Separately

Many primal peoples around the world share a much more interconnected existence than we do in the developed West. In fact, some people in developing countries do not have an identity apart from their tribe. The web of tribal relationships sustains them psychologically and energizes every aspect of their lives. Social researcher Margaret Wheatley states, "In human organizations, a clear sense of identity—of the values, traditions, aspirations, competencies, and culture that guide the operation—is the real source of independence."

The best way to conceptualize a multilocation church is as a web of relationships. It is a tribe. The loyalty is horizontal to your family and peers instead of vertical to the hierarchy and bosses. We share a common DNA. If you could get the entire church together in one place and take a family picture, you would be able to point out family resemblances and relationships—for example, "Those folks used to attend our worship center, but then they left to go start the new group downtown." While the web continues to expand outward, the emphasis is on relationships. Leaders in an organic, multilocation church see themselves at the center of an expanding circle, instead of at the top of a descending pyramid.

How do leaders behave differently in a horizontal organization versus a vertical one?

A few years ago, when it began to be clear that CTK was shaping up differently than any church I'd ever seen before, I was moaning in my office about how I didn't have mentors to show me the way. "I can't think of any other church that is behaving like we are—one church in multiple locations!" A wise staff person (can't remember who it was, actually) said, "Well, aren't we basically doing what Paul did in the New Testament?" (Rim shot followed by dead silence here.)

I went home that afternoon and got out my Bible and started reading Acts and the epistles of Paul with new eyes. What if what Paul was doing back then was actually planting one church, the church of Jesus Christ, in multiple locations? Previously, I had always viewed Paul's ministry through a Western-independent-church-planting lens (that Paul was planting multiple, separate churches). Now I started to see Paul's ministry through an Eastern-interdependent-relationship-expansion lens (that Paul was adding nodes to a network in an ever-expanding circle of relationships). Suddenly the world looked very different to me. But the new lenses also explained a lot. Why was it that believers in Macedonia sent funds to believers in Jerusalem? Maybe because they were all part of the same story. Why was it that Paul was writing letters and still exerting influence in various congregations long after he left them? Maybe because they were all part of the same story. Why was it that a council was convening in Jerusalem and sending a theological statement to believers in Antioch? Maybe because they were all part of the same story. Why was it that the church in various cities was referenced in the singular, "church" instead of "churches"? Maybe because they were all part of the same story. Maybe there was really only one church in the first century, and it met in various places.

I say maybe because we should always let our dogmatism rise and fall with the clarity found in Scripture. Church organization is one of the areas where there is less clarity than we might like. The lack of clarity has given rise to many different church organization models, all of which can in some way find validation from the Bible. But I have to say, as I have looked at the Scriptures, the apostolic organizational model is better than any I've seen to describe what was happening in the early church. It appears to me that the early church was one church that convened cellularly and congregationally in a variety of locations. It was a network tied together by meaningful relationships and meaningful responsibilities.

The first few chapters of Acts tell us that within a few weeks well over 10,000 people had come to Christ and that more people were being added every day. Three times in Acts a reference is made to the church in Jerusalem, and each time it is referred to in the singular. Acts 8:1: "On that day a great persecution broke out against the church at Jerusalem." Acts 11:22: "News of this reached the ears of the church at Jerusalem." Acts 15:4: "When they came to Jerusalem, they were welcomed by the church and the apostles and elders." There is reference to multiple leaders but not to multiple congregations. So what we have in Jerusalem is one church with at least 10,000 adherents, lead by a team of apostles and elders.

Because of its size, it is unlikely that the Jerusalem church gathered as one large group. There was simply no facility that could hold them. Acts 2 tells us they were meeting to hear the apostles' teaching daily "house to house and in the temple courts." The church appears to have been convening in multiple, smaller meetings with multiple teachers. This would mean that every day some portion of the group was meeting, but not the entire group. At the same time, there appears to have been some systemwide solutions provided for meeting the special needs of particular groups (Acts 6) and for theological direction (Acts 15). While Jerusalem was the epicenter, the rings of the church continued out as predicted from Jerusalem, to Judea, to Samaria, to the uttermost parts of the earth. The expansion was facilitated by apostolic journeys, Christian transfers from one region to another (often because of persecution), and circular letters.

Compared with the Western church of the past couple centuries, CTK's organization appears unconventional. But it resonates with the story of the first-century church that we read about in the Bible. I guess we have somewhere to go for guidance after all!

A SENSE OF URGENCY

A man went to his doctor for a checkup. The doctor finally emerged and told him the bad news. "You have only a short time to live." "How long?" he asked. "Ten ..." replied the doctor. "Ten what?" the man asked. "Ten years? Ten months? Ten weeks? Ten days?" "... nine, eight, seven ..."

Beating the Clock

All joking aside — the clock is ticking. In a Deliberately Simple church, there is a sense that time is short. There's a feeling of necessity to act. It comes back to this: hell is hot, and forever is a long, long time. We have a responsibility to reach as many people as we possibly can, as quickly as we possibly can.

The story is told of a dad who had just tucked one of his young sons in bed for the night. As he walked out of the bedroom, he reached for the light switch. His son called out, "Daddy, don't turn on the dark yet!" This is what we pray to our Father too.

The church holds the hope of the world in its hands. The church is a place of salvation. It does not save you; only the gospel saves you. But the church plays a vital role. We carry this good news as a sacred trust. It is our duty to disseminate this truth far and wide. To this end, we are intentional and aggressive in our strategies. Time is precious. There is an urgency about our work. God doesn't want anyone to perish. He wants as many people as possible to accept his offer of salvation (2 Peter 3:9).

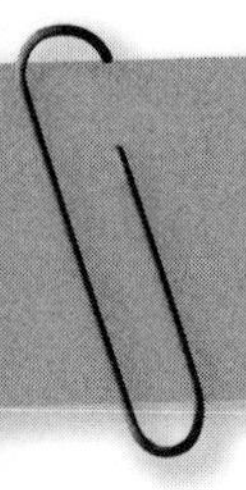

How would you assess your personal urgency toward saving the lost?

"I'm okay, you're okay" complacency produces terminal inaction for churches. We have to get urgency up, fear down, complacency down. We have to get predisposed to go anywhere, to go to anyone, and to go now. "Imminent execution," says Samuel Johnson, "does concentrate the mind wonderfully."

There's an image in the novel *The Catcher in the Rye* where Holden Caulfield, the hero of the novel, dreams that thousands of children are wandering through a field of rye that has grown so high, they can't see they are heading for a cliff. They can't hear Caulfield as he screams to warn them. All he can think to do is run for the cliff's edge and try to catch as many as he can before they fall.

> **ve•loc•i•ty** *n* **1:** the speed at which something moves, happens, or is done **2:** a measure of the rate of change in position of something with respect to time, involving speed and direction

As an outreach church, CTK has an urgency about its message. If there is no hell, there is no reason for us to exist. But if there is a hell, then we have a responsibility to others. The church holds the hope of the world in its hands. The church is a conduit for the life-changing power of God. What is going on in my church is the most important thing happening in the community.

When John Sculley was CEO of Pepsi, he was approached by Apple Computer founder Steve Jobs about coming to Apple. When Sculley resisted, Jobs challenged him, "Do you want to spend the rest of your life selling sugared water, or do you want a chance to change the world?" The question led Sculley to give the next chapter of his life to the computer industry. Yet, as revolutionary as computers have been, nothing can impact our world for time and eternity like the saving grace of Christ.

The power of God is in the gospel (Rom. 1:16). To remain viable, we must stay focused on the life-changing message of Jesus Christ: that God loves us and wants us in his family.

All In

Matthew 25 recounts a story Jesus told of an Oriental master and three servants. The generous master gives the servants varying levels of finances (five talents to the first servant, two talents to the second, and one talent to the third) and then leaves on an extended trip. Because of the context in which this story is told (a discussion about the return of Christ and how we are to live in light of his return), it's clear that the master represents Christ. The three servants represent his disciples. But it is in the details that Jesus really makes his points. First, the master gives the servants a lot of money. A talent, translated across cultures, with inflation, could represent as much as two hundred thousand dollars today. Second, the master gives the trust without restrictions. He basically says, "Here's the money; I'll be back." He doesn't put limitations on the funds. He doesn't even make suggestions for the money's use. But the master does have some assumptions. While he doesn't tell his servants what to do with the money, he assumes they'll do *something*.

The bottom line of the story is that God wants us to be adventurous. He charges us to be entrepreneurs. He challenges us to be creative. He calls us to be aggressive. He invites us to take risks. Jesus' answer to how we are to live in light of his return is, "Go for it!" We're not to wait around. We're to get busy. We're not to wait for instructions. We're to take initiative. We're not to live in fear. We're to proceed in faith.

Hebrews 11 reminds us that without faith it is impossible to please God. Faith feels a lot like risk. Is being a part of Christ's kingdom risky? Yes. There is no safety net. Is it costly? Yes. We seldom have the resources we "need." Is it hard? Yes. But there is a great return on investment.

How does this apply to a Deliberately Simple church? We are the servants who are blessed by a generous Master. We are the ones in a position to do something. You know what we are going to do? We're not going to play it safe. We're going to try to get the greatest return possible. We're going to be aggressive. We're going to stay flexible. We're going to try to reach as many people as we possibly can, as fast as we possibly can. Whatever has been put at our disposal we are going to put in motion for the salvation of others.

I occasionally enjoy watching poker tournaments on television. I don't yet understand all the nuances of the game, but one thing has become apparent to me: the best of the best, when they get the right hand, bet big. Setting aside the morality of gambling (this may be hard for some to do, I understand), the game of poker is a great analogy for church ministry. We all are dealt a hand to play. We have choices to make about how to play that hand. We long for the thrill of victory. We loathe the agony of defeat. And in both poker and ministry, to be successful, you have to be willing to go all in. Jesus says in effect, "I've dealt you a great hand. Now go and play it. I'll be back to pick up my winnings."

> The most effective investment strategy is a highly undiversified portfolio when you are right.
>
> —Jim Collins, *Good to Great*

Doubling Up

An expectation for leaders at CTK is "that you will be growth oriented and plan on serving twice as many people as you presently do. Organize with growth in mind. Plan for the future." This expectation implies that we are pulled by vision instead of pushed by need. We start behaving like a church of one hundred when we are a church of fifty, like a church of one thousand when we are five hundred. This proactivity positions the ministry toward the future and keeps us from accepting the status quo or getting stuck in a rut. An exercise that every pastor should engage in regularly is to take out a piece of paper, write at the top, "My Ministry at Double the Size," and then start to bullet out what that would look like. Would it require an additional service? Additional staff? Reorganization? A different meeting place? Once you know what it would look like, you have ideas about what it will take to get there from here.

The time to plan for the next wave of people is before they come, not after. If you don't have the classes, teachers, parking, or seats for your church to double in size, you probably won't need to worry about it. The 80 percent rule has said that a room feels full at 80 percent, but my experience is that the pressure will build in the parking lot or bathrooms long before that. By thinking double, you can get ahead of the growth curve (and the challenges that always attend growth).

The next horizon is always clearly before us: doubling. A key question to always be asking is, "How can I serve twice as many people as I presently do in the coming year?" Start by assessing your current ministry. For instance, if you currently have responsibility for a worship center that has an attendance of 75 people, the next horizon would be 150. Would serving 150 people require a second service? Start now to plan for that second service, and take some first steps. If you serve in a clerical role and create ten documents a week, how could you get to twenty? Could you recruit a volunteer? Could you standardize some processes? What are your first steps? Identify the key areas you oversee and come up with a plan and first steps toward doubling.

The story Jesus told of the talents implied doubling as an expectation: "The man who had received the five talents brought the other five. 'Master,' he said, 'you entrusted me with five talents. See, I have gained five more'" (Matt. 25:20). Results certainly may vary from the story. We plant and water, and God gives the increase. But in our planning and preparation, we should be getting ready for a 100 percent return on investment.

Doing More

Oskar Schindler, popularized in the movie *Schindler's List*, ran a factory that was a haven for Jews during the Holocaust. At the end of the movie, with the defeat of the Nazis, Schindler walks to his car while the people he has saved line both sides of the street. As he makes his way, he walks by row after row of faces. He is given a letter of thanks, signed by each person, and a ring on which is carved a verse from the Talmud: "He who saves a single life, saves the world." He takes the ring and leans toward Isaac Stern, the factory foreman, and in a voice so low he has to be asked to say it again, says, "I could have done more." He points to his car and his lapel pin (both of which could have been sold to bribe German officials) and breaks down in tears. "I could have done more."

In 2001 the Russian nuclear submarine *Kursk* had a catastrophic accident 350 feet below the surface of the Barents Sea. The enormous vessel—over three football fields long—lay immobilized at the bottom of the ocean. It was five days before the Russian government asked for help for its stranded sailors. When ships finally arrived in the region, their sonar picked up the sounds of sailors banging on the inside of the *Kursk*'s hull. Unfortunately, there was no contingency plan to rescue sailors from a sunken submarine. Slowly the oxygen supplies ran out. The crew was left to die of carbon monoxide poisoning. Their breathing became more rapid, they gasped for air, started to feel severe pain, and then fell unconscious. It was a sad ending. Angry relatives could not understand why the Russian government had not prepared to respond to such an emergency.

What if? What if someone had planned an effective strategy ahead of time? What if they had been ready to go? What if they had responded quickly? What if, instead of the entire crew being lost, the crew had been saved? What if, instead of a funeral filled with mourning, there had been a celebration filled with joy? I don't know. Church? What if?

Do you hear people "banging on the inside of the hull"? Who?

Here, There, Everywhere

The Deliberately Simple church is committed to launching lifeboats—small groups and congregations—here, there, and everywhere. We are not on a pleasure cruise. We are on a rescue mission.

Jesus said, "You will receive power when the Holy Spirit comes on you; and you will be my witnesses in Jerusalem, and in all Judea and Samaria, and to the ends of the earth" (Acts 1:8). In effect he was saying, "Here's what I have in mind for you: circles going out, starting with where you are, going to the surrounding region, extending to adjacent regions, and ultimately taking this message everywhere." Jesus envisioned the church not spinning into the center in a centripetal manner but spinning out from the center in a centrifugal manner. Church is not a place you go to but a place you go from.

> The ragamuffin church is a place of promise and possibility, of adventure and discovery, a community of compassion on the move, strangers and exiles in a foreign land en route to the heavenly Jerusalem. Ragamuffins are a pilgrim people who have checked into the hotel of earth overnight, bags unpacked and ready to go. Regrouping and retrenching, squatting and debating, are not their poses and postures. In their community worship, they reject the insidious inclination to play it safe. The inveterate tendency to entrenchment, which betrays itself in clinging to the tried and true, is accurately discerned as a sign of distrust in the Holy Spirit. The breath of God will not be bottled, and a gallivanting Spirit will not be campused.
>
> —Brennan Manning, *The Ragamuffin Gospel*

As an outreach church, we at CTK are not in the importing business; we are in the exporting business. We don't care who they are or where they are; if they are lost, we want to reach them. We are ready to go. We do not put geographic limitations on where we might go. Jesus asked us not to. "The master told his servant, 'Go out to the roads and country lanes and make them come in, so that my house will be full'" (Luke 14:23).

The Deliberately Simple church will go anywhere to reach anyone. We don't waste time on demographic studies. We don't have a target audience. Jesus already told us to make disciples of all nations and go to the ends of the earth. We don't feel the need to be particularly selective, if he is not going to be.

At Christ the King Community Church we have never done demographic studies prior to launching a small group, café, or center in a community. If there are lost people in the community and leaders willing to reach them, then we figure we need to be there. Here are the groups of people we are trying to get to:

Geographically	Relationally
Close	Close
Close	Distant
Distant	Distant

Starting with those we already know who are near us, we want to work outward to those we don't know who are far from us.

THE FREEDOM TO ACT

Characteristic of Deliberate Simplicity is extreme clarity, not just about priorities but also about pace. Velocity comes not just from a feeling of urgency but also from the freedom to act. One of the truly distinguishing features of a Deliberately Simple church is its ability to move from idea to implementation quickly.

Responsiveness

If time is truly short, then the degree of responsiveness and speed required today is astounding by older standards. At Sony Corporation, the "mean time to prototype" (the elapsed time between the glimmer of an idea and a test of that idea) is a scant five days. Cycle time is now the key. The Deliberately Simple church is built from the bottom up to be flexible and fast, to be highly adaptive to changing environments.

We follow a living, active God. A God who is on the move. The Old Testament tabernacle is a wonderful model of God's presence in the lives of his people. The design was given to Moses by God. The key factor in the tabernacle's design was its mobility. God is not a God who stays put. He's going places. Our challenge is to follow. When the pillar of cloud and fire moves, we move.

A great example of this commitment to flexibility and speed is the story of worldwide courier DHL. DHL stands for the initials of three school buddies (Dalsey, Hillbloom, and Lynn). As a young law student in California, Larry Hillbloom did freelance courier work on the weekends, carrying important documents to Hong Kong or Sidney. On one of his long flights, he dreamed of building a network of individuals who would deliver such documents around the world at a much faster speed than the week to ten days it would often take by standard mail. Without any financial backing, they opened offices in 120 countries in ten years. How did they do it? They built a huge relational network, as Larry Farrell explains in *The Entrepreneurial Age*:

> They started in Asia. On every courier trip each of them took, they signed up somebody to be their local partner—a taxi driver at the Sydney airport, the manager of an A&W Root Beer stand in Malaysia, a toy salesman in Hong Kong. Using this literal seat-of-the-pants approach, the DHL Network began to grow country by country, gaining momentum with each new location. By the late seventies, it was like a thunderbolt roaring across the globe. There were no plans or systems or procedures. Handshakes were the principal contracts. The owner and manager in each DHL outpost was, by default, king of his territory. Each fiefdom had one overriding obligation: "Whatever comes in, and whatever goes out, handle it with the speed of light." Thus was born DHL mini-entrepreneurs—all based on high-speed innovation bordering on the unbelievable.
>
> —Larry C. Farrell, *The Entrepreneurial Age*[11]

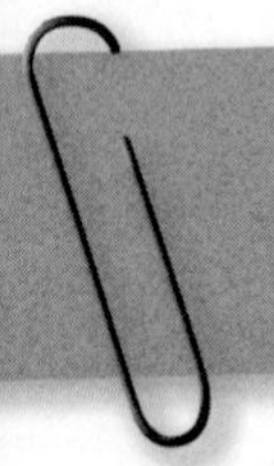

Is the approach DHL has taken transferable to the church? Why or why not?

In his book *Experiencing God*, Henry Blackaby encourages us to "find out where God is at work, and join him in it." We don't go out to save the world, and then ask God to join us. God has already gone out to save the world, and he has already asked us to join him. We are junior partners with almighty God.

Today's the Day

Howard Beckwith, in his book *Selling the Invisible*, tells the story of the first cave dwellers delaying the launch of the wheel. The planning department halts the project, saying, "Delay the launch. We need to wait until man invents vulcanized rubber." It brings to mind the old saying, "He who hesitates is lost." So Beckwith concludes, "Today's good idea almost always will beat tomorrow's better one."

> The consistent lesson I've learned over the years is that I have been in many cases too cautious. I should have torn down the structures sooner, sold off weak businesses faster than I did. Almost everything should and could have been done faster.... When I asked myself, How many times should I have held off on that decision? versus How many times do I wish I'd made that move faster?, I inevitably found that the latter won most of the time.
>
> —Jack Welch, *Straight from the Gut*

At CTK we have gone out and done it and then tried to figure out later how to describe it. We were meeting in more than one location long before we gave thought to being a multilocation church. We have a predisposition toward action. We have not thought our way into a new way of acting; we have acted our way into a new way of thinking. The action-reflection learning model contends that action is the starting point for reflection and therefore fundamental to the learning process.

One of the reasons why the traditional church is so slow is that it is overly concerned with getting it right rather than focused on building momentum. It is more important that we *do the right things* than that we *do things right*. The Deliberately Simple church espouses that fast is better than perfect. Jesus, after all, sent out his followers pretty early in their development and then debriefed them when they came back. This is the pattern that Deliberate Simplicity emulates. Our leader development process is IDTS (identify, deploy, train, support) instead of ITDS (identify, train, deploy, support). We find that deploying first allows us to put leaders into the game more rapidly and creates motivated learners (at least they now have informed questions to ask).

In a church with velocity, there is an impatience that's invigorating. Better to take action and make a mistake than not to take action. In the Deliberately Simple church, there is such urgency that protocol is relaxed. The Deliberately Simple church is the skunk works of the body of Christ—the out-of-the-way, barebones operation where renegades confound the bureaucracy by rapidly implementing outreach ideas.

> Jesus was a real revolutionary, but there doesn't seem to be a whole lot of revolution going on at the moment. There tends to be a whole lot of talk about mission and postmodernism and not a whole lot of direct missional action. While there is a proliferation of books telling us all how to do it, there don't seem to be many working models showing us how to do it. This must change. There needs to be a whole lot more action, and we believe that only in actually doing it will the church discover God in a new way.
>
> —Michael Frost and Alan Hirsch, *The Shaping of Things to Come*

Seth Godin describes a French filmmaking technique, called French hours, that is partly responsible for the very good—and very cheap—movies turned out all the time in France:

> French hours are simple: If every single person on the set agrees, you can film a movie without lunch breaks. They

> serve food (just as much, and probably croissants too) all day long. People eat when they can. The production never slows down. Things move quicker, and efficiency is much higher. The shoot changes to an emergency footing, and the team gets it done as quickly as they can—while still maintaining quality. (Director Joel) Schumacher filmed the thriller *Phone Booth* this way. The entire shoot took 10 days. By contrast, the more average film *Almost Famous* took 92 days. Not only did the esprit de corps and sense of urgency of French hours allow Schumacher to meet his timetable, but they also produced a better movie. The tension in the performance of every actor is palpable. Nobody looks as though he has just eaten a big plate of ziti.[12]

So here's the big question for the church: what does it take to institute "French hours"—not just the lunch thing but an entirely different attitude from the entire body?

FAST INSTEAD OF VAST

The typical church could be described as a large passenger bus. It is designed to hold many people and take them to a common destination. The bus must be driven carefully and take wide turns to get all the people safely to their destination. The Deliberately Simple church, in contrast, could be described as a sports car. It is designed for risk and speed. It is smaller and built to hold only a few people at a time. It can make turns very quickly and responds rapidly to the direction of the driver. If the passenger bus were driven like a sports car, it would likely crash and endanger the lives of all its passengers. If fifty people tried to fit into a sports car, it would slow the car down and probably bring it to a grinding halt.

> If we were honest, we would all acknowledge that it often takes too much time to get things done. Large organizations are like mammoth tankers: the pilot can change course but it takes a long time for the tanker to respond.

> In today's world there's simply not enough time to wait for that change of course. We have to trade in our tankers for tugboats—nippy little workmanlike vessels that can zip in and out of harbor in no time. But there's more to a tugboat than just speed. There's strength, too, strength to pull an idea into port.
>
> —Frank Deprez, *Zero Space*

We live in a culture that is literally moving at the speed of light. Technological advances, such as the internet, have given rise to "net time," a ten-to-one ratio, meaning that business is transacted ten times faster than it was traditionally (even a few years ago). This means that changes that once took ten years to happen are now taking place in one year.

At CTK we like to say that we are fast instead of vast. We have even used the word FAST as an acronym for focused, authentic, strategic, and transferable.

People are often aghast at the speed at which we move. There have been several occasions in which we have launched a new worship center in a community in just a couple weeks. A leader with a passion finds a place to convene some people to worship God, and we say, "Why not?" We know that church planters often have step-by-step processes that take months to execute, but we use the "ready, fire, aim" method.

The world is moving so fast that there are days when the person who says it can't be done is interrupted by the person who is doing it. I once was part of a forum discussion with pastors of multilocation churches. The topic was, "What do you need to have to start a new location?" To my left was a pastor of a leading megachurch in the United States. He said, "We like to have $500,000 for start-up equipment, $1,500,000 to provide financial support for the first two years, a paid staff of 12, and a volunteer staff of 120." The facilitator listed each of these items on the whiteboard. Then he turned to me. I said, "Well, we'd like to have a leader, if we could find one." The facilitator said, "Okay. A leader. That's great!" He wrote, "Leader" on the whiteboard and then turned back for my next point. But I said, "No, that's it. I think that's all we need. If we can find the right leader, the rest of what we need will follow." Jaws dropped around the room at the startling contrast between complexity and simplicity.

Think Big, Act Small

Velocity is the ratio of people reached to people deployed. It is paradoxical that the high growth all pastors want to achieve produces mass and weight, which in turn produces a burgeoning bureaucracy and slower growth. With greater size, complexity grows, and the lethargy of large numbers kicks in.

> High growth gets you size. And the passage of time gets you new leaders. The new leaders are almost always professional managers. These subtle shifts in size and leadership produce a new set of objectives. Presto! Planning, streamlining, and controlling the enterprise become the new order. Managing this and that become more important than making this and selling that. The highest-paid jobs become managing other managers. Meetings, reports, and bureaucracy proliferate on every front. And, slowly but surely, lost in the shuffle are the simple, entrepreneurial basics that got you going in the first place.
>
> —Larry C. Farrell, *The Entrepreneurial Age*

Unfortunately, companies that become large and successful find that maintaining growth becomes progressively more difficult. Numerous studies of company growth statistics have shown that rates diminish swiftly as firms grow in size. Large companies don't experience the dizzying rush of growth that characterizes the first few years. Newer companies grow faster. Smaller companies grow faster. The larger the company, the slower it grows. What emerged from the data is that the factor determining how fast a company grows is its size and little else.

Economists subscribe to the theory that nothing grows to the sky. In other words, no one group can satisfy all demand, because multiple groups can do so much more efficiently. It is better to have small modules of production capacity than a single, high-volume line.

This is congruent with my experience in church growth. To achieve a growth rate of 25 percent when you are a church of eighty means that you reach out to twenty more people and grow to a hundred. To grow at 25 percent when you are a church of two thousand means reaching five hundred more people. Both can be done, but the smaller scenario is often more doable.

> The Rule of 150 says that congregants of a rapidly expanding church ... banking on the epidemic spread of shared ideals need to be particularly cognizant of the perils of bigness. Crossing the 150 line is a small change that can make a big difference.
>
> —Malcolm Gladwell, *The Tipping Point*

As organizations grow, there begin to be structural impediments to the ability of the group to agree and act with one voice. Synchronization of logistics and promotions becomes much more difficult. Lead times become so great that often people choose to leave well enough alone rather than go through a laborious process to bring about a complex change.

Let Leaders Lead

In explaining the difficulty of moving from idea to implementation, experts use terms like "institutional resistance," "bureaucratic stifling," and "inability to capitalize on opportunity." But no matter how you describe it, the root cause is a failure of leadership. Leaders either cannot or do not lead.

The only way to achieve missional velocity is to have leaders —people who are prepared to make smart decisions and implement them efficiently. In fact, at its root the word *lead* comes from an Old English word that means "go, travel, guide." Leaders are goers. They need to be free to travel. They need to be allowed to guide. This means that the organization needs to allow leaders to lead—to have the trust in them that allows them to operate. Allowing people to operate without constantly having to explain themselves enables rapid cognition and response.

> The Special Operations Forces units in the military are replacing their old hierarchical leadership style with something more appropriate for the new roles they find themselves fulfilling. Today soldiers in these units are far more likely to be deployed on a crowded street than in an invasion force. The young soldier confronted with an angry crowd of Bosnian or Haitian citizens doesn't have time to contact his superior for instructions.
>
> —Noel Tichy, *The Leadership Engine*

In the Deliberately Simple church, decisions are made by individuals and then implemented by groups. This is opposite of the traditional church, where decisions are often made by groups (committees, boards) and then carried out by individuals (staff, pastor). And by clarifying the outcomes it is reaching for and simplifying the processes it uses to get there, the Deliberately Simple church makes it easy for people to make decisions without too much thought.

Streamline the Organization

One of the primary reasons why Deliberate Simplicity calls a church to streamline its organization is so it can shed deadweight and achieve greater velocity.

Dell Computers is renowned for its delivery system for personalized computers. They weren't always that good at delivering. But early on, Dell discovered that complexity slowed things down and increased production problems. They cut the number of their core PC suppliers from several hundred to about twenty-five. They standardized critical components, which streamlined their manufacturing. Dell got better and faster by making things simpler.

At CTK one of our fears is getting slowed down. A high value is speed. For this reason, we try to keep teams small and nimble (for instance, our strategic leadership team is four people). It takes time to get people together, to get all their questions answered, to wait for the slowest one in the group. We don't want to organize in a way that needlessly slows us from getting at the harvest.

One of the other dangers in church organizations is the tendency to place people not gifted as leaders in a role in which they are telling people gifted as leaders how to lead. This is the case with some board structures. The pastor, who is a leader, is beholden to board members who are not. Basically, at CTK we've said we want to be led by leaders, not by bean counters. The role of our church council is primarily to insure that I am leading CTK in accordance with our stated mission, vision, and values. Then the authority is mediated relationally throughout the network through our pastors.

At Christ the King Community Church we've felt that if we want to become a movement, we must be able to move. So we've set up a chaordic structure, which combines the maximum *chaotic* behavior with the minimum *order* necessary for stability. Friction, barriers, and boundaries are sources of waste and inefficiency. Keeping it simple helps us to remain flexible. Being chaordic, we have been able to remain agile. Being small pieces loosely joined has allowed us to expand in all directions. Being minimalists in policy and procedures, we have been able to respond to opportunities quickly.

Walk by Faith

The difference between a church characterized by velocity and one that is not is often the difference between faith and fear. It is the line between stepping out and holding back. It is the line between control and empowerment. It is the line between taking action and thinking about it.

When fear gets into a system, it clogs up the works. Decisions come more slowly. Risks get managed. Everyone becomes cautious, calculating, and conservative. Instead of living tiptoe on the edge of expectation, people become hesitant. Eventually we try to protect ourselves, and our passion is gradually restrained, starved, and weakened. We begin to feel less alive as a result. In my opinion, the most fundamental issue holding back the traditional church is, "Are we truly willing to live by faith and risk it … all?" David Wilkerson, in his book *The Dream Giver*, talks about Faith and Ordinary walking down the path together … but faith and ordinary eventually have to part ways.

The only power on earth stronger than fear is faith. We have to believe that God is who he says he is and that he will do what he says he'll do. We cannot believe our eyes. Faith is the substance of things not seen. Faith calls us to go and not to take much in the way of supplies. Faith calls us to put our lives at risk.

A man falls off a cliff but miraculously catches a branch on the way down. He begins yelling, "Is anyone up there?" An answer comes back. "Yes." "Who are you?" "I am God, and I am going to save you." "Wonderful. What should I do?" "Let go of the branch." After a long pause, the man yells, "Is anyone else up there?"

Warren Bennis wrote a book, entitled *Organizing Genius*, in which he looked at leaders who turned around impossible situations. They shared some common traits. Almost always, they were young (thirty-five years young or younger). They had high energy. But they also had an almost delusional confidence. They had no success to protect. Their lack of experience was an asset. They did not know what was supposed to be impossible. They had a completely unrealistic view of what could be accomplished.

Spiritually, we need this. If age, experience, cynicism, and success have robbed us of our pioneering spirit, then we need to return to a vibrant, young faith. The Bible says we can't please God without it. It is also impossible to achieve velocity without it.

Is your "faith age" younger or older than your chronological age?

Respond to Opportunities

The Lord brings opportunities for which you cannot plan. Because of this, we at CTK spend less time in formal planning and goal setting and more time trying to be ready.

> The LORD works out everything for his own ends.... In his heart a man plans his course, but the LORD determines his steps.
>
> —Proverbs 16:4, 9

Our approach to planning at Christ the King is less like a cannonball fired at a fortress and more like a heat-seeking missile tracking a moving target. When the pillar of cloud and fire moves, we'll move with it. We are continually looking for the genius of the Holy Spirit as we chart our course.

Instead of predicting what will happen, we try to find things to exploit. We plan for learning rather than implementation. Instead of forecasts, we feel the need for instant decision-making. Instead of trying to hit goals, we try to increase our willingness to take chances. The importance of speed means a shift from focusing on prediction, foresight, and planning to building in flexibility, courage, and faster reflexes. Intended results and useful tools are more important than a detailed plan. As General George S. Patton observed, "Successful generals make plans to fit circumstances, but do not try to create circumstances to fit plans." This distinction may be particularly important in the kingdom of God, where our plans—no matter how big—are too small for God.

We are attempting something so big that it is doomed to failure unless God is in it. The question we want to ask is not, "Can we afford to do it?" but, "Is it a great thing for God?" We want to let go of the arrogance of knowing and move toward wonder and reverence. We want to move from the black-and-white zone of control toward the gray zone of greater openness.

A lot of planning in churches pushes the present into the future. The better and biblical approach to the future involves prayer and preparation, not prediction.

Long-range planning can be an attempt to turn life into a predictable science. Sometimes complicated plans can be a subconscious attempt to avoid doing, to avoid growing, to avoid faith.

In a Deliberately Simple church, we live with an emotional paradox. On one hand, we revel in the joys of accidental discovery. On the other hand, being human, we don't want to feel out of control. Yet real control is the ability to respond automatically to altered and unpredictable circumstances.

> Enlightened trial and error outperforms the planning of flawless intellects.
>
> —David Kelley

As Scripture instructs us, we want to "keep in step with the Spirit" (Gal. 5:25). Jesus compared the Spirit to the wind—it blows unpredictably. It is critical that we continue to ask, "Where is God at work, and how can we join him in that?"

What are some of the dangers of long-range planning?

Keep from Institutionalizing

Institution. Institutional. Institutionalism. Institutionalization. One of the best questions I get is, "How will CTK keep from institutionalizing?" I hear this question from leaders everywhere—in the U.S., Panama, India, Africa. It is actually comforting to me that so many people are concerned about the same thing. I usually answer, "I'm not sure, but I'm concerned about that too." This would truly be a terrible ending to our story. How do we keep it from happening?

Everything rises and falls with leadership. If we end up becoming institutional, it won't be by accident. Some person or persons will have led us there. If we resist institutionalizing, it won't be by accident either. Some person or persons will have led us there. This is a leadership equation. If we don't want it (and we don't), then leaders everywhere need to root it out whenever it is seen. We must be vigilant. We must l-e-a-d. As small group leaders, ministry directors, and pastors, we are the knights to whom God has entrusted the fair maiden of freedom. What have you done recently to slay the dragon?

The more mavericks, the merrier. I'm not sure we can resist institutionalism better than other organizations have. I certainly wouldn't want to imply that we're better than others who have tried. But I would say that we have certainly acquired a substantial group of mavericks, and this at least gives us a shot. Having personally been a "pharisee of the pharisees" in a previous life, I can smell institutionalization coming from a mile away. I am death on it. There is no way I could ever feel comfortable pastoring a traditional church again. But I am not the only one. Everyone on the church council (which meets with me quarterly) and the strategic leadership team (which meets with me monthly) stands with me in this. None of us want to go there, and that rebellion toward institutionalism is one of the main reasons we're here.

The time to fight institutionalization is early and often. You don't wait until it is full grown. You oppose it in its infancy. What are the early warning signs that we are beginning to calcify? The arrows start pointing in instead of out. We start getting more concerned about stuff than about people. The people start supporting the leaders in their ministries instead of the leaders supporting the people in theirs. Program creep: instead of trying to reach people organically through relationship, we start trying to reach them attractionally through programming. Sniff. Sniff. Sniff. Do you smell smoke? If you do, sound the alarm.

One of the best antidotes to institutionalism that I see in our story is decentralization. Decentralization is our friend. We have now infected leaders on various continents with the virus. Even if a group of people build up immunity to the infection, it is likely that the epidemic will continue to spread through other carriers. Actually, our story is already moving at a much faster rate in places like Africa and India than in the United States. So if leaders in one part of the world won't resist institutionalism, leaders somewhere else will. And even if we wanted to stop the ideas from spreading, we couldn't, because we have no centralized control, only relational influence.

There is a tendency to come out of every problem we encounter and write a policy to keep that from happening again. We have to resist this urge to legislate. We will have to deal with our share of problems, to be sure. Every organization has to deal with their share of problems. But we want to deal with them in a different way than the average institution does. We want to solve problems relationally. Personally. Not through policy and writ. Frankly, it is chicken and lazy to sit at your computer, write policy, and stick the paper in everyone's in-box. Anyone can do it, which is why it is done so often. But the better though harder way is to sit down with people and talk with them. Sometimes writing things down is a good thing. But let's make sure that anything on paper is a bridge to get people where they want to go instead of a barrier to keep them from getting there. And then let's make sure the paper shredder is working.

This fear of institutionalism is real. We have an enemy, and I'm sure he's scheming right now to ruin this story. If I were him, I would see institutionalization as a strategic weapon. Listen, it's not paranoia when they're really out to get you! Because of the real threat of institutionalization, I proposed in our original bylaws that we have a drop-dead date at ten years—that is, that we would cease to exist as an organization exactly ten years after we were formed. The church council at that time appreciated the sentiment but thought this was a bad idea because people would become nervous and distracted as the date approached (for example, would you want to be hired by an organization that was going to drop dead in the next year?). So here's what I decided to do instead. At the ten-year anniversary of our first service, April 4, 2009 (and every five years after that), I will be conducting an informal review, asking, "Is God still at work in this story?" This will be a question I put out to the entire body, and I will be looking for candid, real feedback and examples to support their answer. If the answer turns out to be no, I hope we will have the courage to face reality. None of us want to perpetuate a lifeless organization, least of all me.

Spiritual ends require spiritual means. If we want to see a vibrant, powerful movement, in which we are keeping the main thing the main thing, staying out of God's way, being extremely sensitive to the Spirit's promptings, deploying leaders around the world, "paying it forward," and unleashing the church, we are asking for a miracle. Really, all that is miraculous. People have already proven people can't do it. But God can. Everything good that has happened in the CTK story to date has happened in response to prayer. If we want even greater things to happen, we must pray with greater fervency than ever.

SCATTERING

My journey of Deliberate Simplicity has ended up being a wild ride. What began as a small group in a small valley has multiplied into a worldwide minimovement of small groups and worship centers in various counties, states, and countries. I could never have predicted when we started out that Christ the King Community Church would go where it has gone and do what it has done.

For instance, a chapter of the CTK story began in India when Yedidya Parker found a Christ the King T-shirt in a used clothing bin on the streets of Hyderabad. Having seen the magnitude of that city (6.5 million people), it is a "needle in a haystack" miracle that a man with a call from God to rapidly expand his kingdom would find this shirt. Today, largely as a result of Yedidya's leadership, the CTK story has spread throughout Inida, and CTK's logo is seen not just on shirts but also on church buildings, trucks, motorcycles, and handbags.

Yedidya is a modern-day apostle who has preached in over a thousand villages, places where the gospel had never been preached before. He has baptized thousands of converts. He has deployed scores of evangelists and pastors. He is courageous though regularly threatened for his witness by both the Hindu and Muslim population. He is revered throughout the country as a man of God who gives himself sacrificially. He follows in the footsteps of his godly father, Abraham Parker, who pastored for many years in Hyderabad in spite of persecution and hardship. Yedidya is the greatest legacy of his father's ministry, as he is now raising up hundreds of leaders in his wake. Many of the leaders with whom Yedidya is working are dynamic in their own right. And all this from a single T-shirt!

One day I was sitting in my office with Paul Evanson. Paul is CTK's first small group leader in the Skagit Valley, so he and I have had front-row seats to this entire story. We know each other well enough to know that neither of us could take credit for this. It is clearly a God thing. So in a quiet moment I asked him, "Why do you suppose that God has blessed CTK like he has?" His response was insightful. "I think it's because we have kept the arrows pointed out. And when the arrows are pointed out, it aligns itself with the heart of God, and he is pleased to bless that." He had no sooner said that than I reached for a three-by-five card and wrote on it, "arrow pointed out." Prior to that I had never heard a phrase that so succinctly captured CTK's story.

There were two parts to Paul's answer: what we are doing, and how God feels about that. The first part is indisputable. We have kept the arrows pointed out. When we started CTK, we told the first participants that we were not going to ask everyone to come to us. We were going to ask us to go to them. And we have made good on that. For the most part, CTK is not the kind of church you go to but the kind of church you go from.

But the second part of the answer needs some research. Paul said, "When the arrows are pointed out, it aligns itself with the heart of God, and he is pleased to bless that." Really?

An "Arrows Out" Theology

Does God care which way the arrows are pointed? Does it matter to him whether we gather or scatter? Whether we stay or go? Our investigation into God's point of view begins at the ancient Tower of Babel.

> Now the whole world had one language and a common speech. As men moved eastward, they found a plain in Shinar and *settled* there.
>
> They said to each other, "Come, let's make bricks and bake them thoroughly." They used brick instead of stone, and tar for mortar. Then they said, "Come, let us build ourselves a city, with a tower that reaches to the heavens, so that we may make a name for ourselves and *not be scattered* over the face of the whole earth."
>
> But the LORD came down to see the city and the tower that the men were building. The LORD said, "If as one people speaking the same language they have begun to do this, then nothing they plan to do will be impossible for them. Come, let us go down and confuse their language so they will not understand each other."
>
> *So the LORD scattered them* from there over all the earth, and they stopped building the city. That is why it was called Babel—because there the LORD confused the language of the whole world. From there *the LORD scattered them* over the face of the whole earth.
>
> —Genesis 11:1–9, emphases added

Genesis 11 records a conflict in agenda between God and people. Humankind's agenda was to settle and not be scattered. It was to build walls and towers, to go vertical instead of horizontal. God's agenda was quite opposite. It was for people to scatter instead of gather.

"Arrows out" was God's first command to humankind, as evidenced by his earliest recorded statements to Adam and Eve.

At the beginning of the Bible, we read, "God blessed them and said to them, 'Be fruitful and increase in number; fill the earth and subdue it'" (Gen. 1:28). Some feel that God's first command was to have children. But that is actually a means to an end. God's primary command was to fill the earth. God said in effect, "Take my blessings and propagate them everywhere." For that to happen, there obviously had to be more than just two people on the planet. So God said, "Have kids and spread yourselves around."

It didn't go down like that. If anything was propagated, it was evil, not God's rule and reign. So God pressed the restart button with a worldwide flood and started over with Noah. His first words to Noah and his family when they came off the ark and set foot on dry ground echoed God's original directive.

> Then God blessed Noah and his sons, saying to them, "Be fruitful and increase in number and fill the earth."
>
> —Genesis 9:1

Two chapters later we find ourselves at the Tower of Babel. The people went east a little ways, but not too far. They settled and started to build a tower. So while "Arrows out" was God's command to humanity, people were more interested in gathering than scattering.

> Babel is the human attempt to deal with sin by being together.
>
> —Mark Driscoll

Babel became the site of the ancient city of Babylon and the basis of a worldview that is seen in contrast to God throughout Scripture. The Babylonian mentality was to be self-reliant and self-protective. To hunker down. God's command was to move out. To leave the compound. But humankind has historically settled, chosen comfort over cause, built towers and walls, and not fulfilled the potential of walking by faith.

So after a false start with Adam, a failed restart with Noah, and the debacle of Babel, God narrowed his focus to just one man, Abraham.

> The LORD had said to Abram, "Leave your country, your people and your father's household and go to the land I will show you. I will make you into a great nation and I will bless you; I will make your name great, and you will be a blessing. I will bless those who bless you, and whoever curses you I will curse; and *all peoples on earth will be blessed* through you."
>
> —Genesis 12:1–3, emphasis added

"Arrows out" was God's call to Abraham. God's agenda is still the same. Leave the ranch. Go. Be a blessing. All peoples on earth.

> The greatest heresy of monotheism is cherishing clause A of the Abrahamic covenant while conveniently suppressing, ignoring or forgetting clause B. Clause A says we will be blessed—that God will make us great. Clause B says that is so that we can bless the world, and make the world great.
>
> —Leslie Newbigin

There is an Eastern story of four men who, while crossing a desert, come upon a compound surrounded with high walls. The first one scales the wall, lets out a whoop and jumps over. The second and third ones follow suit. The fourth man gets to the top of the wall and sees below him an enchanted garden with sparkling streams, pleasant groves, and luscious fruit. Though longing to jump over, he resists the temptation. Remembering other wayfarers who are traveling the burning desert, he climbs back down and devotes himself to directing them to the oasis.

"Arrows out" was God's call to Abraham's descendants, but Israel was more interested in being blessed than in being a blessing. So "Arrows out" became God's commission to the church.

> *Go* and make disciples of all nations, baptizing them in the name of the Father and of the Son and of the Holy Spirit, and teaching them to obey everything I have commanded you. And surely I am with you always, to the very end of the age.
>
> —Matthew 28:19–20, emphasis added

God's agenda was repeated. Go. All nations. God's commission to the church was, "Arrows out." The church, unfortunately, has instead had the arrows pointed in. For the most part, we do church as if the gospel commission were given to the lost, telling them to come to our churches. The Great Commission does not say come; it says go. But we create events, programs, services, and classes, then hope and pray that people will come to us.

The gospel says, "Seek the lost," but our buildings and advertising say, "Stay." The gospel says, "Seek the lost," but our pastors and programs say, "Let the lost seek the church." Particularly in modernity, the church has communicated to nonbelievers, "There are blessings to being on the inside. You're on the outside, so you can't enjoy them. Want to be blessed like us? Get on the inside!" The church has largely failed to go outside the walls to spread the blessings. We have largely ignored the advice of Dallas Willard: "In a pluralistic world, a religion is valued by the benefits it brings to non-adherents."

> The church is trying to get out of what God is trying to get into—the world. We have churches full of people who love Jesus, but who don't love what Jesus loves.
>
> —Leonard Sweet

There are two tensions in a church—outreach and nurture. Without intentionality, nurture always wins. Through the years, I've come to realize that I need correctional lenses for my heart. I will always want to have my needs met before I concern myself with meeting the needs of others.

G. K. Chesterton talked about how the symbol of many of the world's religions is a circle. It is closed. It is concentrated. On the other hand, he said, "the cross ... can extend its four arms forever without altering its shape.... The cross opens its arms to the four winds." As Christians, we are to go forth under the banner of the cross—arrows out in all directions.

What steps does a church need to take to make sure outreach doesn't get choked off by nurture?

Flipping the Script

Left to ourselves, Christians quickly circle the wagons. We build towers and walls. We look to be blessed instead of being a blessing. I say "left to ourselves" because God's last, best effort to help us get the arrows pointed out was to send his Spirit to indwell us. God's answer to Babel is Pentecost.

> You will receive power when the Holy Spirit comes on you; and you will be my witnesses in Jerusalem, and in all Judea and Samaria, and *to the ends of the earth.*
>
> —Acts 1:8, emphasis added

Once again God's agenda is clear. Jerusalem. Then Judea. Then Samaria. Then the ends of the earth. Arrows out. Pentecost is the reversal of Babel. Pentecost represents the heart of God. At Pentecost, instead of Babylonian gathering we see Spirit-inspired scattering.

Babel	Pentecost
Vertical	Horizontal
Going up	Going out
Gathering	Scattering
Confused tongues	Anointed tongues
Can't understand	Every person hears

Jesus' desire to see the message go out may explain his departure from earth. Brennan Manning theorizes, "The mystery of Jesus' ascension into heaven contains an important lesson. He said to His disciples: 'I am telling you the truth: it is for your own good that I am going' (John 16:7). Why? How could Jesus' departure profit the apostles? Because while He was still visible on earth, there was the danger they would be too wedded to the sight of His flesh."[13] By decentralizing God's presence within us, God prepares the way to achieving his original agenda: "all people on earth will be blessed."

DISSEMINATION

Can the church think forward and outward instead of inward and backward? Can we start thinking about those we are to serve instead of how they can serve us? Michael Frost and Alan Hirsch, in their book *The Shaping of Things to Come*, question the "Arrows in" approach of many churches: "How much of the traditional church's energy goes into adjusting their programs and their public meetings to cater to an unseen constituency? If we get our seating, our parking, our children's program, our preaching, and our music right, they will come. This assumes that we have a place in our society and that people don't join our churches because, though they want to be Christians, they're unhappy with the product." Deliberate Simplicity is an attempt to reverse the flow from importing to exporting—from trying to get them to come to us to trying to get us to go to them.

Juan Carlos Ortiz, who has had a huge impact in Latin America, saw his ministry expand along with his "prayer maps." He began by praying over a map of his community. Then he started praying over a map of his city. Then a map of his region. Then a map of South America. How big is the map you are praying over?

John Byrne is a well-known writer who focuses on current business practices. He has put forth ten questions to assess a company's greatness:

1. Does your company create an emotional bond with its customers?
2. Does your strategy stand out from the crowd?
3. Is your company a fun place to work—a fun organization to do business with?
4. Are you built to change?
5. Do you embrace the value of values?
6. Are you as disciplined as you are creative?
7. Are you winning the battle for talent?
8. Do you use technology to change expectations and reshape your business?
9. Are you built for speed?
10. Have you built a company of leaders?

A nice list of questions, for business or church leaders, but Byrne feels it is incomplete. He says that while there are companies that meet every one of these tests, yet there is still one more—perhaps the most important and most difficult of all:

11. Can you scale?

Byrne has seen many companies that were very functional and effective yet failed to scale their processes and organization for broader impact. The traditional church has not had a very good answer to question 11.

scal•able *adj*: capable of being scaled

scale *n*: a succession or progression of steps or degrees; the proportion that a representation of an object bears to the object itself

How is it that Christianity can become a world-changing movement? It's pretty simple, if we want to be deliberate about it.

> Be strong in the grace that is in Christ Jesus. And the things you have heard me say in the presence of many witnesses entrust to reliable men who will also be qualified to teach others.
>
> —2 Timothy 2:1–2

Transferability

Transferability makes possible the rapid advancement of Christ's kingdom. Paul says to Timothy that first we must be strong in the grace that is in Christ. That is not always easy. There will always be individuals and institutions which will make us think that we are not good enough—that we don't measure up. But once we are strengthened in grace, we are to take the things that God has given to us and entrust them to others. That is, we are to hand off the baton, make it transferable.

Studies indicate that a single shaft of wheat, if allowed to reproduce and grow, could expand into a crop large enough to feed the world within eight years.

This has application for us as individuals and as a church. Our task is to multiply believers, leaders, groups, services, and sites. We all should be looking to replicate ourselves. If we are willing to decentralize the ministry, what Jesus prophesied in Acts 1:8 could come true.

> You will receive power when the Holy Spirit comes on you; and you will be my witnesses in Jerusalem, and in all Judea and Samaria, and to the ends of the earth.
>
> —Acts 1:8

The traditional church has been engaged in near and far missions, and nothing in between. Jesus saw the church as rings going out—from where they were, to the surrounding region, to the adjacent region, to the farthest spots on earth. What this speaks to is a church that is replicating itself. It's a church that is into not just addition but also multiplication.

The most rapid way for a church to replicate is to subscribe to the KISS method: keep it simple and scalable. One of the most devastating computer viruses in history had only 356 bits of information. The code was so small that it replicated easily and spread rapidly over the internet. Once, when I was visiting some of our CTK leaders in Africa, I was apologizing that much of our web-based training was not functional for them, since they do not have broadband access. The response of one of the leaders was instructive. He said, "That's no problem. The story is so simple, we can tell it."

In order to replicate, jobs need to be achievable. The organization must be understandable. Processes need to be transferable. Simplicity is required if a church wants to spawn a movement in which thousands are actively engaged in the ministry, instead of a select, seminary-trained few. So as we look at our organizational structure, our systems, and our methods, a chief concern is simplicity. We keep asking, "Is there a simpler way to do this?" A scalable church needs transferable ideals, clear descriptions, repeatable procedures, disseminated information, and a supportive structure.

Ideas and relationships define a Deliberately Simple church. Because of that, such a church can expand quickly. Ideas can be conveyed and grasped as quickly as synapses can fire. Relationships can be formed and maintained over long distances. Intangibles don't cost anything to transport and can be moved quickly.

Repeatability

When Ray Kroc secured the master franchising rights to McDonald's, he didn't go to work in a McDonald's restaurant.

He went to work on the McDonald's business. To Kroc, the first McDonald's restaurant was just a model or prototype that could be reproduced again and again in cities and towns all over the world.

Instead of personally rolling up his sleeves to run the joint, he began analyzing every operational function of the original McDonald's, from purchasing and prep to cooking and cleaning. Without changing the essence of the concept, he made refinements and proceeded to develop a comprehensive set of standards and procedures, essentially a system for running a hamburger stand "the McDonald's way." He told his franchisees that following his system would allow them to give their customers the same experience his customers had at the original McDonald's and give the franchisee the same experience he had as an owner. And it worked! Kroc scaled McDonald's into an efficient system that could be reliably and quickly reproduced. He was a pioneer of organizational repeatability.

"Relentless repeatability" was a phrase used by golf legend Ben Hogan to describe the driving force behind his professional success. Repeatability is the essence of mastery, control, speed, and reliability. A relentlessly repeatable formula can have powerful implications.

Pastor Sid Porter says, "If you want 1000 pounds of meat, raise elephants. If you want 1000 tons of meat, raise rabbits." If you put two elephants in a room and two rabbits in a room, in three years you will have three elephants and 476 million rabbits.

Elephants	**Rabbits**
Only fertile four times a year	Almost continuously fertile
Only one per pregnancy	Average seven per pregnancy

Twenty-two-month gestation period	One-month gestation period
Sexual maturity at eighteen years	Sexual maturity at four months

Deliberate Simplicity asks, "With all these elephants around, isn't it time for a rabbit plague?"

Is it time for a rabbit plague?

CELLULAR

Unterror Cells

Deliberate Simplicity advocates a cellular approach to transforming the spiritual landscape. We actually have a very good (but bad) example of what we're talking about in the terrorist networks that have (unfortunately) changed our world (Al-Qaeda, Hezbola, etc.). In a recent *Leadership* magazine article, Brian McLaren beautifully expands on this analogy:

> I can't stop thinking of faith communities as "unterror cells." While terror cells plot violence to spread fear, faith cells plot goodness to spread hope. Both want change; both see status quo as unacceptable. But terror networks believe change is pushed by fear and violence; faith networks believe constructive change is pulled by hope and love, service and friendship.
>
> Recently I heard someone describe terror networks. All nodes of the network innovate, he said, and all nodes coordinate to share their innovations. In this way all nodes

> influence the direction of the network as a whole, and any node can lead. They move like a flock of birds, school of fish, or swarm of bees, and they can respond to changes quickly. All nodes recruit, too, and all nodes share a common and clearly defined enemy—an enemy big enough and bad enough (in their minds) to keep them tightly unified.
>
> What would happen if more of us saw our faith communities—churches, small groups, circle of friends, monastic communities, mission teams, whatever—as nodes in an unterror network that was constantly plotting goodness and hope?
>
> And what if more pastors saw it not as a desk job but as an integral mission, where we are supported by our churches to be pastors for our communities? What if we saw ourselves as leaders of a global unterror network?
>
> Could our denominations reinvent themselves, transforming from systems of control and homogenization to diverse networks linking unterror nodes for communication, coordination, innovation, inspiration, mutual influence?
>
> What is the real enemy we're striving against? And what is the hope we're striving for? What's preventing us from moving together like a flock of birds? What kinds of young men and women would be attracted to this kind of life—as unterrorists, networked in subversion of every unjust and apathetic status quo?... What if the pastorate really is a non-office job, and the local church an unterror cell?[14]

I think McLaren pretty well summarized what we are trying to be and do at CTK.

Organic Multiplication

By building the ministry around relationships, the Deliberately Simple church is able to grow organically, naturally, more like a plant than a machine. In the story of the first-century church, we read, "All the believers were together and had everything in common. Selling their possessions and goods, they gave to anyone as he had need" (Acts 2:44–45). In the first century, people were getting their needs met. How? Was the church developing a program or a department to meet the needs? No, they simply noticed that their brother or sister had a need and responded to it. Organically. People were meeting together. They were finding out what the needs were. And they were responding to them as they had ability. It was that simple. They were behaving more like an organism than an organization.

Organization	Organism
Growth by addition	Growth by multiplication
Energy from outside	Energy from within
Dead	Alive
Expansion caused	Expansion natural

In an organization, growth is by addition. If you want a bigger machine, you have to add more parts. In an organism, growth is by multiplication. The cells continuously divide, sometimes into very small parts, and multiply. In an organism, cells regenerate and grow naturally.

Organisms are alive, with inherent energy. Organizations, on the other hand, are dead. You need to plug the machine into an electric outlet or fill it with gasoline for it to run.

Christ's kingdom is an organism. Its expansion is natural. In a Deliberately Simple church, we have made a commitment to have the minimal organization necessary to support life, rather than to try to inject life into lifeless organization.

Christ described his kingdom as an organism. In Matthew 13 Jesus tells several parables about the kingdom—analogies meant to help us understand a new dynamic. He speaks of farmers spreading seeds, seeds landing on various kinds of soil, and yeast making its way through dough. Many of his stories bring to mind images of reproduction and scalability. Growth and reproduction are built in. "This is how it is in my kingdom," Jesus basically says.

Organic does not mean without structure. Organisms characteristically have a very definable skeleton—joints, branches, capillaries, and the like. The body of Christ, likewise, is well connected and supported. When speaking of Christ's body, the apostle Paul referred to "supporting ligament[s]" in Ephesians 4:16 and "ligaments and sinews" in Colossians 2:19. A ligament connects a bone to another bone; a sinew, or tendon, connects a muscle to a bone. I think what Paul was saying is that in the body of Christ there are people who help hold things together, who keep things from falling apart.

Organic does not mean small. In nature, the big exists to support the small (exactly opposite of most organizational models, in which the small exists to support the big). Bigger bones support smaller bones. Bigger muscles support smaller muscles. And the connections are made through the ligaments and tendons. In the CTK story, we have been blessed because larger, established worship centers have "paid it forward" to assist small-sized centers, not just with resources but with prayer, relationships, people power, and coaching. It reminds me of how, in the forest, smaller flora and fauna will not survive except for the shade and protection of the larger trees. We need all sizes working in a supportive ecosystem. This is why at CTK, while we always want to validate the small, we can't forget to appreciate the big, and the ligaments and tendons that hold it all together.

Michael Frost and Alan Hirsch capture the essence of organic life in their book *The Shaping of Things to Come*. They contend that "reproducibility is innate to all biological systems. One need look no further than to our own bodies or to the nearest tree. Part of the fundamental aim of all living systems is to ensure a progeny in some form or another. The apple tree produces fruit, and at the heart of the fruit is a cluster of seeds. In the seed there is everything present to produce future apple trees." The potential of such systems is staggering. As has been said, "Anyone can count the seeds in an apple, but only God can count the number of apples in a seed."

The church of Jesus Christ has not been nearly as viral as Jesus described. Early on it was, when it was meeting house to house and in the temple courts. But it didn't take long for bureaucracy to set in. The medieval church took an approach that was more organizational than organic, as has today's corporate church.

> Reproduction is not hard. It is natural. Dare I say, it is even pleasurable.... Inbred in all living things is a desire to reproduce. It drives us. Today you will be faced with advertising and images that appeal to your own sexuality, which is what causes reproduction. Sex is everywhere, because it is so important to us (granted, a little too important to us). The fact that reproduction is thought to be so hard and painful for churches is evidence of how far removed we are from being healthy and natural.
>
> —Neil Cole, *Organic Church*

In organic life there is always repetition and revelation. That is, organisms express both similarity and uniqueness. In an organic church there is self-similarity in terms of mission, vision, and values but differentiation in personality. As we say at CTK, "If you've seen one CTK worship center, you've seen one CTK worship center." And yet in every one of our locations, you have the sense that "this is CTK."

An organic approach to the church means that inside each of us lies the seed of a church. The driving force behind a viral church is not the professional clergy but Christ operating within every one of us.

Leader Deployment

At Christ the King Community Church our ministry is defined by relationships, not by geography. We are attempting to see groups, cafés, and centers established here, there, and everywhere. We believe that we can go as far as relationships will take us.

Our strategy is to multiply groups by multiplying leaders. We have come to the conclusion that we are not in the church growth business. We are not in the church planting business. We are not in the multisite business. We are in the leader deployment business.

The kind of leader we are looking for is a "pastorpreneur." A pastorpreneur (pastor/entrepreneur) is a kingdom-minded leader who has a heart for people and the ingenuity to reach them. A pastorpreneur has received from God both the heart and head, the sensitivity and skills, to make a difference. Pastorpreneurs are so concerned about reaching lost people that they will launch a new ministry endeavor to save them.

> There are many ministers among us. Most of them do not work for a church.
>
> —Carl George

By multiplying leaders, a Deliberately Simple church multiplies impact and fuels the rapid expansion of Christ's kingdom. We can reach an unlimited number of people if we can deploy an unlimited number of leaders. Our process for multiplying leaders is IDTS: identify, deploy, train, support. Deploy first, then train. After we identify leaders, we want to deploy them. Once they are in the game, we train and support them as they influence others.

In the first century, the apostle Paul would enter a pagan community and several weeks later appoint elders from among the converts to provide spiritual leadership in his absence. Elders in our modern context are typically individuals with years of spiritual maturity and Christian understanding. But perhaps we have made it more complicated than it needs to be. From the New Testament, it appears that in a matter of weeks you can know what you need to know to be a fully devoted follower of Christ.

In Romania today, fifteen hundred organized churches will meet to worship Christ. What is phenomenal about this is that there are only about 120 pastors for those fifteen hundred churches. Most pastors serve four to seven churches. Many churches don't have a pastor at all. Yet all these churches are growing rapidly. It is a testament to what Christians can do if leaders get out of their way.

The focus of a pastorpreneur is balanced between the process and the people. The process is the ministry; the people are the ministers. If the pastorpreneur is too focused on the process and ignores the people, it will not work. On the other hand, if he or she is too people-centric and does not facilitate the process well, it will not work either. Pastorpreneurs must be able to deal with both people and things skillfully.

Do you consider yourself a pastorpreneur? Why or why not? If not, do you know someone who is one?

Not all pastors are pastorpreneurs. The difference between a pastor and a pastorpreneur might be the difference between an employee and an owner. A pastorpreneur is self-inspired and self-directed to fulfill God's calling on his or her life. A pastorpreneur has an obsession to pursue his or her sense of mission and to make a difference in the expansion of Christ's kingdom. A pastorpreneur is comfortable being a trendsetter rather than a replicator.

Replicators	Trendsetters
Prefer predictability	Favor unpredictability that invites imagination
Avoid the risk of change	Believe the greatest risk is waiting until circumstances force change
Are managers who wish to preserve the past	Are leaders who shape the future
Look for evidence that something works and fear making mistakes	Treat mistakes as an integral part of the experimentation necessary for doing anything original
React to trends	Anticipate trends and accelerate them
Look for agreement and view deviation as dangerous	Do what others consider "going too far" and see conformity as dangerous
Base strategy on giving people what they request	Give people what they had never thought of asking for
Rely on proven answers	Raise provocative questions that accelerate learning

Pastorpreneurs decide to become a part of the CTK story for several reasons: they are inspired by our ministry philosophy (mission, vision, values, etc.), they want to be connected to us relationally, or they sense it is a God thing. The model we use at CTK to engage pastorpreneurs is very relational. In some ways, it resembles a dating relationship. We begin with introductions. We start interacting, dating, and courting. We eventually get engaged and married. We join together in a vision to see a prevailing multilocation church emerge that will transform the spiritual landscape.

MOVEMENT

There are choices to be made in ministry. Choices between inward focus and outward focus. Between developing a great ministry and developing a great movement. A Deliberately Simple church makes its choices clear: to be outward focused ... to be a movement instead of a ministry.

I make a slight distinction between a movement and a network. All movements are a network, but not all networks are movements. A movement must be decentralized, self-replicating, and empowering. A network could just be into broadcasting—"big jug, little mug." A network beats a single station, but nothing beats a movement.

Plug and Play

The failure of Apple computer to achieve greater market share for its platform by moving to an open architecture is well documented. The Macintosh operating system, though superior, was proprietary and controlled. Thus the Microsoft/PC platform became the accepted and scalable system for the masses. But Apple was not the only casualty to old-line, command-and-control thinking.

> Among those who ignored the tide and clung to their old-line industry maps was IBM. At first it appeared that IBM was embracing the PC revolution. Its PC machines were among the hottest-selling in the market. But deep down, IBM fundamentally misunderstood the new shape of the industry. Grove, who personally witnessed the revolution as a supplier to IBM, says the company was "composed of a group of people who had won time and time again, decade after decade, in the battle among vertical computer

> players. The managers who ran IBM grew up in this world. When the industry changed, they attempted to use the same type of thinking regarding product development and competitiveness that had worked so well in the past." As an example, Grove cites the development of the OS/2. This operating system was technically outstanding. However, IBM didn't see the importance that open architecture and interchangeability had come to play in making PC's attractive to customers, so it was painfully slow in making OS/2 available for computers from other manufacturers. It took almost three years to sell 600,000 copies of OS/2 (of which very few were used), while Microsoft only needed ten months to sell approximately 13 million copies of Windows 3.0. When IBM finally decided to make aggressive changes to OS/2, it was too late. Microsoft had captured people's imagination with Windows. OS/2 was a dismal failure, and a waste of money for IBM.
>
> —Noel Tichy, *The Leadership Engine*[15]

The dream for Christ the King Community Church is to provide an opportunity for pastorpreneurial leaders to "plug and play." That is, if you align with the mission, vision, values, beliefs, and priorities of CTK, then you can engage immediately with us in the work. It's that simple.

There is no future for hermetically sealed, closed systems in a world full of networks. What a network can give us, through connectivity, speed, and intangibles, is increasing returns instead of diminishing ones. As it grows, it is able to become more efficient instead of less.

Infinity and Beyond

Leaders who subscribe to the factors of Deliberate Simplicity—minimality, intentionality, reality, multility, velocity, scalability—are in a long line of pioneers and explorers. Like Captain Cook, Magellan, and Lewis and Clark, they feel a need "to boldly go." They would prefer to risk rather than settle. This pioneering spirit seems to be an expression of the image of God in us.

One organization with which a Deliberately Simple church can relate is the National Aeronautics and Space Administration (NASA). Both the church and NASA are charged to go. And both the church and NASA have had their share of challenges. After some catastrophic equipment failures at NASA (most notably the *Challenger* disaster), someone editorialized,

> Our problems must be solved, but not at the expense of exploration. Exploration is not a luxury. It defines us as a civilization. It directly or indirectly benefits every member of society. It yields an inspirational dividend whose impact on our self-image, confidence, and economic and geopolitical stature is immeasurable.

That statement reminds us that something bigger is going on here. I've taken that statement and tweaked it as a mandate for the church:

> Our [church] problems must be solved, but not at the expense of exploration [reaching out]. Exploration [outreach] is not a luxury. It defines us as a civilization [church]. It directly or indirectly benefits every member of society [the world]. It yields an inspirational dividend whose impact on our self-image, confidence, and economic and geopolitical stature is immeasurable [we are blessed and it's a lot of fun when the arrows are pointed out and we are aligned with our Creator's agenda].

CONCLUSION

It's an Equation

$$< \; = \; - \; \times \; + \; \infty$$

Deliberate Simplicity is a new equation for church development. It purports that less is more, and more is better. It is a system of thought and behavior that yields a definable outcome: a church that is nimble, responsive, and expanding.

Systems thinking explores the loops and links of group dynamics. It says that things are interrelated. A system takes its integrity and form from the ongoing interaction of its parts. Systems are defined by the fact that their elements have a common purpose and behave in common ways, precisely because they are interrelated toward that purpose.

A systems thinking mantra is, "Your system is perfectly designed to produce the result you're getting." If you are manufacturing cars and every third car rolls off the assembly line missing a right front fender, your system is perfectly designed to produce that result. Also, if you remove aspects of the system or change them, you will alter the results.

An illustration of the importance of the parts to the whole in a system is the DC-3, the first commercially viable airplane. The

Wright brothers proved that powered flight was possible, but the McDonnell Douglas DC-3, introduced in 1935, ushered in the era of commercial air travel.

The DC-3 was the first plane that supported itself economically as well as aerodynamically. Other, earlier planes were not reliable and cost-effective on an appropriate scale. The DC-3 for the first time brought together five critical components:

- The variable-pitch propeller
- Retractable landing gear
- Lightweight, molded body construction
- Radial, air-cooled engine
- Wing flaps

To succeed, the DC-3 needed all five; four were not enough. One year earlier the Boeing 247 was introduced with all the components except wing flaps. Because the plane lacked wing flaps, Boeing engineers found that it was unstable on takeoff and landing, and they had to downsize the engine.

In a similar way, Deliberate Simplicity is an interdependent system that requires all six factors for maximum performance. If you subscribe to multility without minimality, you will replicate complexity and, in the end, frustration. If you subscribe to intentionality without reality, you will produce an inauthentic expression of Christ's kingdom—you will get better and better at being phony. If you subscribe to scalability without velocity, you will aspire to be a movement but won't be able to move.

Deliberate Simplicity requires all six elements in the equation. But when you have the six elements, you have the potential to become an authentic Christian community that effectively reaches out to unchurched people in love, acceptance, and forgiveness so they may experience the joy of salvation and a purposeful life of discipleship. With Deliberate Simplicity, you can see a prevailing, multilocation church emerge that will transform the spiritual landscape. This church will convene in hundreds of small groups with worship centers strategically located in every community.

What are your takeaways from Deliberate Simplicity? What steps will you take to incorporate the six factors of the Deliberate Simplicity concept?

I value your thoughts about what you've just read. Please share them with me. You'll find contact information in the back of this book.

NOTES

INTRODUCTION

1. Donald E. Miller, *Reinventing American Protestantism* (Berkeley, CA: Univ. of California Press, 1999), 20.
2. Len Lewis, *The Trader Joe's Adventure: Turning a Unique Approach to Business into a Retailing and Cultural Phenomenon* (Chicago: Dearborn Trade, 2005), x, 20.
3. Jim Collins, *Good to Great: Why Some Companies Make the Leap . . . and Others Don't* (New York: Harper Collins, 2001), 158–59.

MINIMALITY

4. Kennon L. Callahan, *Small, Strong Congregations: Creating Strengths and Health for Your Congregation* (San Francisco: Jossey-Bass, 2000), 25–26.
5. Bill Breen, "Rapid Motion," *Fast Company* (August 2001), 106.
6. Linda Temple, "McMansion Passion Is Diminishing," *USA Today* (May 16, 2003), D8.

INTENTIONALITY

7. Kennon L. Callahan, *Small, Strong Congregations: Creating Strengths and Health for Your Congregation* (San Francisco: Jossey-Bass, 2000), 236–37.

REALITY

8. F. B. Meyer, "Where Is It?" www.sermonindex.net, accessed August 8, 2008.
9. Brennan Manning, *The Ragamuffin Gospel* (Sisters, OR: Multnomah, 1999), 174–75.

MULTILITY

10. Lyle Schaller, *Discontinuity and Hope* (Nashville: Abingdon, 1999), 174–75.

VELOCITY

11. Larry C. Farrell, *The Entrepreneurial Age* (New York: Allworth, 2001), 180.
12. Seth Godin, "Changing," *Fast Company* (August 2004), 93.

SCALABILITY

13. Brennan Manning, *The Ragamuffin Gospel* (Sisters, OR: Multnomah, 1990), 116.
14. Brian McLaren, "Leader's Insight: Unterror Cells," Leadership Journal.net (September 11, 2006), http://www.christianitytoday.com/leaders/newsletter/2006/cln60911.html. Copyright 2006 Brian McLaren and Christianity Today International. Reprinted by permission of *Leadership* journal, www.leadershipjournal.net.
15. Noel M. Tichy, *The Leadership Engine: How Winning Companies Build Leaders at Every Level* (New York: HarperCollins, 1997), 30.

For more information on Deliberate Simplicity, including resources, coaching, and seminars, go to www.deliberatesimplicity.com. You may also download the following free bonus articles from the site:

Seven Ways Less Can Be More
Tewenty-Five Reasons to Be Multisite
Organic Site Development Process
Short and Sweet—The One Hour Service
Differences—What Makes CTK Different

You can view Dave Browning's blog at www.deliberate simplicity.blogspot.com.

For more information:

www.ctkonline.com
888-421-4CTK
info@ctkonline.com

Sticky Church

Author: Larry Osborne

In *Sticky Church*, author and pastor Larry Osborne makes the case that closing the back door of your church is even more important than opening the front door wider. He offers a time-tested strategy for doing so: sermon-based small groups that dig deeper into the weekend message and Velcro™ members to the ministry. It's a strategy that enabled Osborne's congregation to grow from a handful of people to one of the larger churches in the nation—without any marketing or special programming.

Sticky Church tells the inspiring story of North Coast Church's phenomenal growth and offers practical tips for launching your own sermon-based small group ministry.

Sticky Church is an ideal book for church leaders who want to start or retool their small group ministry—and Velcro™ their congregation to the Bible and each other.

Softcover: 978-0-310-28508-3

Leadership Network Innovation Series, The

The Monkey and the Fish

Liquid Leadership for a Third-Culture Church

Dave Gibbons

We need fresh, creative counterintuitive ways of doing ministry and leading the church in the twenty-first century. We need to adapt. Fast. Both in our practices and our thinking.

The aim of this book is simple: When we understand the powerful forces at work in the world today, we'll learn how something called third culture can yield perhaps the most critical missing ingredient in the church—adaptability—and help the church remain on the best side of history.

A third-culture church and a third-culture leader look at our new global village and the church's role in that village in a revolutionary way. Third culture is a way to reconnect with the historical roots of what Jesus envisioned the church could be—a people known for a brand of love, unity, goodness, and extravagant spirit that defies all conventions.

Softcover: 978-0-310-27602-9

Share Your Thoughts

With the Author: Your comments will be forwarded to the author when you send them to *zauthor@zondervan.com.*

With Zondervan: Submit your review of this book by writing to *zreview@zondervan.com.*

Free Online Resources at www.zondervan.com/hello

Zondervan AuthorTracker: Be notified whenever your favorite authors publish new books, go on tour, or post an update about what's happening in their lives.

Daily Bible Verses and Devotions: Enrich your life with daily Bible verses or devotions that help you start every morning focused on God.

Free Email Publications: Sign up for newsletters on fiction, Christian living, church ministry, parenting, and more.

Zondervan Bible Search: Find and compare Bible passages in a variety of translations at www.zondervanbiblesearch.com.

Other Benefits: Register yourself to receive online benefits like coupons and special offers, or to participate in research.